THE CHILDHOOD OF JESUS

THE CHILDHOOD OF JESUS

Paul Sédir

FRIENDS
IN SPIRIT

First published in French as
L'Enfance de Christ
Bibliothéque Universelle Beaudelot, 1914
First English edition © Friends in Spirit, 2024
an imprint of Sophia Perennis
Translation © Friends in Spirit 2024
Series Editor: James R. Wetmore

All rights reserved

No part of this book may be reproduced or transmitted,
in any form or by any means, without permission

For information, address:
Friends in Spirit
Box 931, Philmont, NY 12565

ISBN 978-1-59731-223-3 (pbk)
ISBN 978-1-59731-224-0 (cloth)

Cover Design: Michael Schrauzer

CONTENTS

Biographical Sketch i
Foreword 1
The Body of the Gospels 3
The Gospel in the Invisible World 31
The Genealogy of Jesus 48
John the Baptist 60
Elijah 74
The Virgin 88
The Trinity 107
The Parents of Jesus 138
The Magnificat 159
The Canticle of Zacharias 171
Bethlehem 181
The Presentation 198
The Word 210
The Birth of the Word Within Us 226
The Childhood 238
Conclusion 247

Acknowledgments

The publisher is deeply indebted to the "friends" of *Les Amitiés Spirituelles*, who have kept Paul Sédir's books in print in French for over a century, and for the dedication of those who have nurtured the vision that one day these books might appear in worthy editions for Anglophone readers. We gratefully thank in this connection Piers Vaughn and Peter Urbanski for the exchange of textual materials many years ago that led to this presents series, Robert Ledwidge for his technical assistance, and especially Madame Zadah Guérin-McCaffery, who nurtured this same vision and worked towards its realization for decades. Her skilled devotion to Sédir's works helped ensure that Sédir's carefully crafted style has been preserved in these Friends in Spirit translations.

Biographical Sketch

VON LE LOUP, son of Hippolyte Le Loup and Séraphine Foeller, was born on January 2, 1871 in Dinan, in the Côtes du Nord region of France. As a child, Yvon suffered the effects of tuberculosis, partial blindness, and a grave leg fracture that troubled him throughout his life. His mother, of Hessian origin, taught him German, which he later spoke fluently. At the age of nine, he made his First Communion at St Augustin's church, then entered the Jesuit school on rue des Francs Bourgeois, where he quickly distinguished himself by his great intelligence. Observant to a fault, he became a fine draughtsman and would have liked to paint. He was drawn to music, drawing, literature, and was extraordinarily dexterous with his hands. In due course, however, he was obliged to pursue a more practical academic course, owing to the influence of his father, an old soldier imbued with discipline who had little understanding for the refinement of this quiet child with lofty aspirations. And so, as soon a Yvon passed his academic exams (1892), he joined the Banque de France. He was twenty-one years old.

A few years earlier, in his late teens (around 1890), a profound shift in Yvon's orientation had taken shape. Not far from the Banque de France was an esoteric bookshop and publishing house (La Librairie du Merveilleux), where Yvon soon met the well-known writer on esoteric matters, Dr. Gerard Encausse (Papus). This led to a great friendship between the two quite different men. Papus set the young Yvon to work organizing his extensive esoteric library and introduced him to numerous personalities from the heady, even feverish, esoteric milieu of the time. One evening, he was taken to the home of Stanislas de Guaita, a nobleman of Italian descent who possessed the most complete esoteric library then in existence. Around this time, Yvon published an article ("An Experiment in Practical Occultism") and made his debut as a speaker on the theme: "Divinatory Sciences and Chiromancy."

In 1891, Papus had formed the Order of Martinists, based on the teachings of "The Unknown Philosopher," Louis Claude de Saint-Martin (1743–1803), and asked Yvon to collaborate. This fraternity took up the ideas of Martinez de Pasqually's Kabbalistic rite, and formed the first initiatory level of Guaita's Rosicrucian fraternity. In these circles, young authors frequently used pseudonyms. Yvon took the name Paul Sédir (anagram of désir), Gerard Encausse became Papus, Dr. Emmanuel Lalande used the name Marc Haven, etc. From the time of his association with the new Martinist Order, Yvon regularly published his work as Paul Sédir.

In 1895, Papus passed his doctorate in medicine and opened a home for the aged. This necessitated Sédir taking on the bulk of the esoteric-hermetic activities on which he and Papus had been collaborating. Every evening he gave classes in Hebrew and Sanskrit, the psychic training of Hindu fakirs, yoga, experimental alchemy, astrology, esoteric botany, etc. He also organized various research groups on related subjects.

Sédir was also much attracted to mysticism, and frequented literary circles such that of the poet Paul-Marie

Biographical Sketch

Verlaine. Meanwhile, in the rue de l'Ancienne Comédie, meetings of the Martinist Order were taking place, where Sédir became acquainted with individuals engaged in experiments regarding which he would later say: "It is here-below that you pay the highest price." His alchemical research did, however, enable him to acquire an ever deeper understanding of the foundations of what is known as the Great Work.

All these early aspects of Sédir's esoteric life reveal an overarching quest for truth that always led him to first experience something before speaking about it. He had by now attained great heights of "secret" knowledge, and even power. But to his great good fortune he had the wisdom to detach himself from these as soon as he realized their worthlessness and danger.

In July 1897, Gerard Encausse arranged for Sédir (then 26 years old) to meet a most singular man, Master Philippe of Lyon (Nizier Anthelme Philippe), to whom he was introduced by Madame Encausse. Master Philippe was a remarkable healer whom Sédir and others in his circle considered a Christian Master of the highest degree. Shortly after this meeting, Sédir left for Lyon to spend his vacation there. Just what happened at that time remains a private matter, although Sédir gives some inkling of what transpired in his autobiographical book *Initiations*, and also in a remarkable letter of May 1910:

> Together with some companions, I have done the rounds of all esotericisms and explored all crypts with the most fervent sincerity and hope of success. But none of the certainties I eventually grasped appeared

THE CHILDHOOD OF JESUS

to be The Certainty. Rabbis communicated their secret manuscripts to me; alchemists admitted me to their laboratories; Sufis, Buddhists, and Taoists led me during long nights to the abodes of their gods; a Brahmin let me copy his tables of mantra; a yogi imparted to me the secrets of contemplation. But one evening, after a certain meeting, what these admirable men taught became for me like haze rising at dusk on a sultry day. We run after what we think is hidden, but know nothing of our own religion, though its dogma and liturgy are the most complete presentation of integral knowledge on earth. Everything is there in Christianity. The Hindu *trimurti* is neither the Christian trinity nor the Pythagorean ternary; gnosis and the gospels do not lead to the same goal. Read in the texts what is there, not what one would wish to find there. To see that we know nothing; to experience that we can do nothing; to verify that heaven is here within us, and that our Friend constantly enfolds us within his blessed arms—this is the lesson of Jesus. This I have attempted to say by publishing, among other works, five volumes of lectures on the gospels.

Master Philippe had changed Sédir's orientation. *His mission had been affirmed.* He gave up all the esoteric fraternities (and his various ranks and offices in them) in order to devote himself wholly to living and spreading the gospel. His commentaries on the life of Christ are especially notable in that he accepts the intuitive faculty as a means of approaching the Truth. Sédir's literary output was extensive. His best known works are from this period are: *Prayer, Initiations, Mystic Forces, Christian Mysticism, Seven Mystical Gardens, The Childhood of Jesus, The Sermon on the Mount,*

Biographical Sketch

Some Friends of God, The Healings of Christ, The Kingdom of God, The Crowning of His Work, Weekly Meditations, and *The Incandescent Path.* His lectures and books drew many devoted students, and in due course a fellowship called Les Amitiés Spirituelles ("Friends in Spirit") was formed. This organization undertook to publish many of Sédir's books, and though it is much diminished, it remains active today.

Sédir died in Paris. Twenty years later, Breton poet and novelist Théophile Briant of Dinan wrote:

> On February 3, 1926, Paul Sédir died in Paris at the age of 55. The death of this admirable man, with his gospel-inspired heart, went almost unnoticed by the mainstream press, which was more preoccupied with crowning the charlatans and histrionics who were entertaining the public, even as international catastrophes were on the verge of breaking out. Apart from the chosen few whom this Apostle of the End Times had called to the Light, most post-war jabberers were unaware that one of the century's most eloquent voices was no longer to be heard. His was a forerunner's voice, the voice of a herald proclaiming in a wilderness of contentious crowds, a voice that had been devoted for years to spreading the gospel and, at the threshold of the abyss, was raised in dire warning against the multiplied prostitutions of the word.[†]

[†] This sketch is based on biographical materials provided by Émile Besson and Max Camis (close friends of Sédir), recently published in English in *Paul Sédir: His Life and Work* (Friends in Spirit, 2024).

Foreword

HOSE who possess some knowledge of esoteric or religious doctrines, and who for the past thirty years have honored me by reading my books, have been surprised at some of my affirmations. Many have asked me from what source I had drawn. My answers were expressed orally, and only to those of whose unshakable convictions I was certain. But I owe a few words of explanation to other sincere searchers. In the Foreword of the first edition I stated that the ideas I expounded were not my own:

> The one who gave them to me will forgive me if I have involuntarily deformed his light; the omissions and errors are mine. May all the good that his teaching gave me, and that which it may still produce, return to him in spite of the incompetence of the interpreter.

I renew that declaration with all the power I possess, but still will not designate the one to whom I owe everything. It might be construed and said that my silence is an adroit ingratitude. I accept that misconception. I will continue to keep silent in order to preserve a great number of metaphysicians from profound slanders (the results of which are formidable), to shield the work of my master from premature publicity, and finally, to keep him from being held responsible for my errors.

People at large too often lack the sense of critical evaluation. It is hard for them to make allowances for personal equations. They rationalize, beg the question, often lack logic. Moreover, he who taught me possesses the very rare gift called the "gift of tongues," which theologians have failed to sufficiently explain. For instance, if an orator speaking French has made himself understood to a cosmopolitan audience that understands none but their own tongues, he possesses the gift of tongues. But he who, addressing himself to his compatriots, is understood differently by each individual according to their personal needs and capacities—that one too possesses the gift of tongues.[1]

As for myself, a disciple, the only lights I have been able to capture as I read the gospel and listened to the words of my master were those he considered necessary for me to have. Am I presumptuous? Dare I believe that I have understood him thoroughly, or even heard him correctly? Would I pretend with vanity to place the result of my studies under the shadow of his name? He, who sees right into my heart, knows full well if I am trying to mount a pedestal. And he knows quite well how to bring to himself those who will have read my particular commentaries upon his universal word. Although certain persons seem to want to force me into making formal statements, for these and other reasons I will still keep silent.

The Precursor, John the Baptist, declared himself unworthy to unloose the latchet of Christ's sandals. Who am I in comparison to the greatest among the children of men? May those who read my books keep all their emotion, all their enthusiasm, for him who is their only Master since the creation of their souls, and who will remain their Friend unto eternity.

[1] To understand the language of plants, of animals, and of the invisible is a third form of the gift of tongues. And there are still others.

The Body of the Gospels

Dogmas—Exegesis—Modernism—Miracles—Inner Viewpoint—The Two Exegeses—Their Future Concordance—Differences Among the Four Gospels—The Identity of Jesus—The Supernatural World—The Evangelists—Their Symbols—The Messiah—Correspondences—The Adepts—Christic Initiation—Method of Study

VERYONE KNOWS that the libertarian movement of human intellect, born of the Reformation, grew under the deism of the 18th century, and has thereafter blossomed under the guise of modernism. As against this stands the immovable figure of Catholic orthodoxy founded upon St Thomas Aquinas. His *Summa* is not an encyclopedia. As its name indicates, it is an immense library that theologians augment little by little. Its files are sufficient to hold all the applications that the Church has made, or will make, from its fundamental dogmas. The basis of the *Summa* is the "Treatise of the True Religion" wherein St Thomas anchors Catholicism upon two columns—the Scriptures and the Church—and upholds its teachings upon the Councils, the Fathers, and the Theologians. In the magnificent didacticism of the Angelic Doctor, one notices that he maintains that everything can be proven by reason. In this, he is an Aristotelian. Yet reason cannot prove what is supernatural (that supernatural with which the Scriptures are saturated). It can only

prove it negatively. That is what the modernists headed by Littre say. The only proof of the supernatural they might concede and admit to is a miracle. Yet they have never been able to find a definite, authentic, scientifically-proven miracle. Hence they presume that, as a miracle does not exist, neither does the supernatural. If the Scriptures are not of supernatural origin, Catholicism is not divine anymore, but merely human.

On the other hand, exegesis teaches us that in the books of the Old and New Testaments there are contradictions, fables, historical errors, and interpolations. Father Richard Simon and Sylvestre de Sacy noted this long ago, and who hasn't read the stentorian declarations of the Abbé Loisy and of Ernest Renan? What answer does one give to a philologist who proves that the Messianic prophecies of the Psalms are false? That the book of Daniel is an apocrypha composed at the time of Antiochus Epiphanes? That St Matthew's gospel is a compilation of various stories strung end to end? That Jesus was not born in Bethlehem, that he was not of the family of David, and that St John's gospel is an Alexandrine transplant?

Intellectuals have always had a closed mind regarding miracles. They carry within themselves a tenacious idolatry of the laws of matter that persists even after profound inner perturbations. Thus, in the charming *Life of St Francis of Assisi* that Jorgensen has written, we find that he has interpreted the anecdote of the wolf of Gubbio as merely symbolizing a social event. Mr. Jorgensen is an artist who was converted to Catholicism by the aesthetic side of that religion, but he is also a scholar and a philosopher. Certain aspects of that life escape him: he cannot conceive how an animal may understand a saint. To him, it is an impossibil-

The Body of the Gospels

ity. His intelligence follows an *a priori*. That the too celebrated author of the *Life of Jesus* considers St Francis of Assisi to be extravagant, or St Theresa to be an hysteric, is conceivable enough, given that his professor of psychology was Charcot. As for all the psychics who consider the saints and Christ as mediums, magnetists, or magi—they are transcendental materialists or occultists as well, because for them the supernatural does not exist. They have not yet distinguished between phenomena owing to an unknown force of nature, and a miracle due to God's direct intervention. They will have to understand first that all marvels do not come from a pure source, just as theologians will some day have to admit that all marvels do not stem from the devil. It will be necessary to study the natural history of the Invisible. We will have to recognize that the Invisible is a universe beyond us, parallel to our unconscious. William James, Émile Boutroux, and Henri Bergson are paving the way for the minds of man to comprehend this. I only wish they would proclaim the traditional and mystical origin of their ideas. If one feels the truth on these two points (the existence of the created Invisible and the existence of the Uncreated), then all the discussions between exegetes and apologists lose their reason for being. It is then one notices that it is not the letter but the spirit of the Scriptures that is true.

What does it really matter whether the gospel stories are but tales retold inaccurately by uneducated people devoid of imagination? What does it matter if John seems to borrow from Philo? Might it not be Philo of Alexandria who translates Christic metaphysics into Platonic language? Didn't Jesus speak all sorts of tongues? The expressions "Word," "Son of God," "Light," and "Union" are abstract

THE CHILDHOOD OF JESUS

only to a philosopher, but for the mystic they are concrete realities. Ernest Renan may declare with some insinuating thoughts in the back of his mind that Jesus was not educated, that he did not know Philo or the Greeks or the Talmud; that he was an ordinary man, simple-minded and superstitious, unsystematic—but who possessed a formidable will power surpassing any previously known. Renan may claim that the beauty and charm of the gospels are but the reflection of the beauties of Galilee, that Jesus was not a thaumaturgist, that such miracles as the Last Supper and the Resurrection are but symbolic legends; that Buddhism and the Talmud already contain most of the maxims and gospel parables, that Jesus was strongly under the influence of the Precursor (the latter being himself influenced by the Sabists of Babylon)... As I said, though Renan tries to insinuate that the true post-mortem life of Christ is the memory he left in the heart of mankind, though he interprets all texts according to the thesis that makes of Jesus a man just like us, thus following the trend of the 18th-century philosophers and Fabre d'Olivet (preceding Tolstoy and our modern esotericists)—Renan the Grand Master of contemporary skepticism is obliged to admit that "a profound plan seemingly wished to hide the traces of the great founder, both historically and topographically."

It is true that Jesus has always shown himself to be indifferent to history, to renown, to any material accuracy in books, documents, and science. He was the opposite of the wise men and kings who write or erect commemorative monuments to themselves. It seems as though he meant to scorn the means by which men cultivate glory, and the sacrifices they offer to the gods of terrestrial renown. Just as he knew everything without ever having ransacked library shelves, his disregard for methods of knowledge might, rather, reveal to us that true knowledge is to be found within, in the spirit, in the living union with truth.

It is evident that an intellectual won't understand such an apparent lack of method. With this in mind, it would be exact to say with Renan that "the Fathers and theologians were less Christian," because they systematized, defined, limited. But in truth, the Word of Jesus is as vast as the world, and as limitless in its applications as the infinite crowds of creatures to whom it is addressed.

Evidently, however, a component of personal equation does enter into the sacred texts. Apologetics rightly teaches that it was the Spirit who dictated to writers, but that the writers have not always been faithful. Moreover, there are the inevitable accidents of transmission, catastrophes, and fraudulent maneuvers attempted for a spiritual or political end. Just as Christ permitted his body to be tortured, so has he permitted his thought to be truncated, though in a lesser measure. So the disciple needs not fear science. In fact, the detections of "criticism" and its variations show him how an invisible reality becomes altered upon becoming visible.

Yes, Christ spoke. How did his audience hear and interpret his words? How did the Councils understand and establish them? Did the Holy Spirit enlighten them? Yes, but within the measure that these theologians were able to receive his Light—because to pretend that an unworthy heart may be as filled with God as a saintly one would be an admission that God at times violates our liberty.

Eusebius of Caesarea and St Jerome state that the finale of the second gospel and the verse of the adulteress in St

John were not in the ancient or authenticated manuscripts. And it is true that they seem to be omitted. The verse of the three celestial witnesses (First Epistle of John) has always remained completely unknown to the Greek tradition (and to the Latin tradition until the 4th century). However, in 1897 the Congregation of the Holy Office declared it to be authentic. It is needless to enumerate more such divergences.

For his part, the Abbé Loisy proves to be quite reasonable, it seems to me, when he explains:

> The Vulgate, as far as it represents the primitive Scriptures, has to a theologian the authoritative aspect of an inspired text; as far as the version composed with the approval of the Church by men permeated with its teachings, then approved and adopted by the Councils and the Popes and consecrated by liturgical usage, it still bears the authority of a traditional source. The Church, to make use of it with full confidence, need not check in detail, from the translation, that which conforms to the original texts and that which differs from them by omission, addition, or modification; between what was in the hagiographer's thought and what the translators might have added under the influence of her own tradition.

Bossuet (*Discours sur L'Histoire Universelle*, part II, ch. 27), and with him all theologians, believe that each sacred book is produced by its author under divine inspiration and kept "without one iota being altered by a reverential posterity." Richard Simon, forefather of the modernists, sees in tradition the work of successive generations that improve and enrich the original manuscript. In the East, a book is

The Body of the Gospels

really a collective work. Even the name of the author is often symbolic, such as Hermes, Zoroaster, and Manu.

I might even say from the mystical point of view that it does not seem to be God's method to ever limit our liberty thus. He gives us lights. Never does he use coercive means to prevent us from modifying them. The Father prefers that we use our free will within the limits wherein our digressions may only cause temporary inconveniences. These differences, even those that seem condemnable and damnable, often serve an unknown purpose. What we should do is to conciliate through an inner act of submission the exuberance of our liberty with an acquiescence to the providential designs. This act is called prayer. And any intellectual work (even that of erudition) would improve infinitely, were it conceived in prayer and published with prayers.

⊕

Where is the system that lasts fifty years? As a case in point: science, historical criticism, faith, and Catholic dogma (which are actually at opposing poles) will be conciliated the day that they recognize having different domains. The visible and the invisible, the subjective and the objective, matter and force—all the dualities—have a common origin, it is true. But this origin is not one of the terms of the binaries—it is a third term, still unknown.

Regarding the three synoptic gospels Matthew, Mark, and Luke, the critics agree today that Mark is the source from which Matthew and Luke have borrowed. That might well be, but it leaves me indifferent. That there might have been an original gospel in Hebrew by Matthew, and other sources also (since Luke declares that others had written before him), that there might have been two or three transmitters

THE CHILDHOOD OF JESUS

between Christ and our versions of the gospel—all that is quite probable, especially if, having been a member of some occult group or other, one remembers and notes how the words of an initiator are amplified or restricted (distorted in any case) after merely a few years of transmission, no matter how respectfully or convincingly it was done.

Moreover, the fourth gospel, which St Irenaeus attests the diffusion thereof about AD 180, differs from the three others on the historical angle. Also, it depicts a very different Jesus. It speaks of the Word. Yet the modernists, who are intellectuals, see in this gospel, as I said before, Neoplatonic philosophy and symbols—even within the miracles and in the historical narratives. Critical study of the fourth gospel has given birth to the gravest discussions, to doubts of the most pernicious kind, and to affirmations most dangerous for the spiritual health of man. This becomes the breeding ground of philosophical modernism, a ground enclaved primarily in the domain of Protestantism, and which all the singular doctrines derived from ancient Eastern esotericisms try to enlarge—a peat-bogged ground blooming with poisonous plants, where I see multitudes being sucked in to be fatally asphyxiated.

Paul, the disciple of Gamaliel, says: "The Savior, who existed in heaven in the form of God, thought it not robbery to be equal with God; but made himself of no reputation, and took upon himself the form of a servant, and was made in the likeness of man." (Philippians 2:6–7)

Peter said: "Jesus of Nazareth, a man approved of God.... This Jesus whom God raised up ... God has made Christ and Lord, this Jesus whom you have crucified and slain." (Acts 2:22–24; 10:38–40) Disquieting words for him who seeks to find God in Jesus.

The Body of the Gospels

It is possible that the disciples may have recognized Jesus as Son of God only after having seen him resurrected. It is also possible that a few may have known spiritually who he was as soon as they met him, though out of prudence and respect they never mentioned it. Most of the time Jesus states that he is Son of Man and Messiah. Now, the dogma of divinity is indemonstrable. It is purely an element of faith. The intellectual minds of the time followed the emanationist theory of the Logos. Our contemporary intellectuals regard St John's Gospel as mystical pantheism. But the mystic finds in it a rectification, or rather destruction, of pantheism and the illustration of this old axiom in its purest sense: "Everything is alive."

As far as I have been able to fathom, Paul sees Jesus as the Perfect Man having descended to help humankind in distress (I Corinthians 15:47). John sees Jesus as the threefold Word: divine, cosmic, psychic. The Church has blended the two concepts. She has declared that the Word and the Holy Spirit are persons really distinct from the Father, that the Word is consubstantial to the Father and is not (as per Arius) just first among creatures.

How are the two natures of Christ *connected*? Is he personally eternal? Is he the soul of the man Jesus, as Apollinaire claims? No, answers the Church: he was a complete man. Hence, concludes Nestorius, he must be a man united to the divine Word. Neither. Christ is ONE (a total unity). Then, queries Eutyches, his human nature must be fused into his divine nature? Oh, no, replies the Council of Chalcedony: the two natures coexist. To which the Fifth Ecumenical Council adds that the human nature is substantially united to the Word and subsists in the Word. Finally, the Sixth Council decrees Christ to be a unity of persons, a duality of natures, of wills, and of *modus operandi*.

⊕

It seems as though, in this dogma, theologians have gathered together challenges to philosophical reasoning. I, however, think they have given the best indication in the world of how one must contemplate the most incomprehensible of all mysteries. This universal mystery is to be found at the base of any science, and is indemonstrable *a priori*. Henri Poincare hereupon made remarks that are correct, which he explained in a language accessible to men of average culture—I mean the question of Christ Jesus as the question of creation, for our Savior contains all the impossibles and all the inconceivables. It is the superiority of our religion to proclaim him God and man. The other systems that see him only as an evolved man overshadowed by the Holy Spirit and thus as evolvable, thereby prove that they are incomplete in spite of their highly philosophical aspect.

The psychology of Christ is as incomprehensible to the psychologists as it is also to the "initiates." Neither admit the existence of the supernatural. They believe only in a more or less sublime and subtle "natural" state. They never will conceive that the Spirit of God, Absolute Life, *ipso facto* commands all matter (even the most radiant) and all relative life (even the most glorious).

On the other hand, for motives indiscernible to us, Jesus speaks, acts, and operates sometimes as a man, sometimes as God. The duality of his outer manifestation must have been one of the most painful works of his mission. It is indispensable that the reader of the gospel learn how to differentiate between these delicate distinctions.

The Body of the Gospels

Let us recapitulate.

A critical examination of the texts does not interest us. If those among my readers who are not Catholic are not frightened by my daring, I must also remind the Catholics that revelation is not dogma. There were no dogmas in the first centuries—yet all were servants of all. Dogmas are necessary and useful parapets, but alas! the human species is all too fertile in illuminati. How few really examine their personal intuitions under the beam of sane reason? Rarer are those who strive towards moral perfection before wishfully hoping to receive some new inner truth.

To conclude, the requisite is sincerity, because God is magnanimous and he always gives to the sincere soul the means of extricating itself from error. To know the total truth, let us live according to the partial truth that our conscience, education, and instruction indicate to us. It will not be Catholics alone who will enter into the Kingdom. I do not know the details of the Council's edicts upon that. But I know that in the Book of the Law that is placed upon the Throne of the Lamb, it stands written: Any man who loves his neighbor as himself will be saved.

The word "gospel" signified simultaneously good news, the messenger of this news, and the sacrifice of the expressions of gratitude offered to the gods.

The four evangelical accounts have existed since the beginning of the Christian era. Tertullian and Clement of Alexandria mention it (cf. *Diatessaron* of Tatian). According to St Irenaeus, Origen, and Muratori, the order in which they are actually found (Matthew, Mark, Luke, John) follows their seniority.

THE CHILDHOOD OF JESUS

Matthew's gospel was written about AD 42 in Syrian Aramaic and then translated into Alexandrian Greek or Hellenistic dialect. It stemmed from accounts gathered in northeast Palestine, in the country of the Galileans, where some relatives of Jesus were still residing, so it seems, in the second century (Papias of Hierapolis, AD 130).

Mark's gospel, written in AD 52 and dictated by the Prince of the Apostles, addressed itself to the Romans. According to tradition, Mark was the nephew of St Barnabas, the friend of Philo the Jew, and evangelized Lower Egypt.

Luke (Lucanus of Antioch) was a pagan converted to Christianity, says St Jerome. He was a painter according to both Simeon the Metaphrast (10th century) and St Thomas Aquinas; a doctor, according to popular tradition. He died in Ephesus. His work has been accepted by exegetes and is recognized as having the greatest historical value.

John, whose name in Hebrew means "Jehovah favors him," wrote only when he was ninety, in the year 100 of our Christian era. All theologians, from St Ambrose, St Leon, and Notker down to the Greek Church, consider him the most illumined. His gospel must have been the work of his autumn.

I will not enter into any details of exegesis. All these apologetical and critical studies are useful only for the rational or scholarly study of the texts—and such is not my aim. It is the spirit within the core of the gospel that we will attempt to penetrate. That is why I will lay aside many commentaries that would interest the curiosity seekers of occultism, of the Kabbalah, and of Theosophy.

The Body of the Gospels

⊕

The symbols attributed to the evangelists are first recorded by St Ambrose; St Jerome, and St Gregory the Great. Johann Reuchlin (*De Arte Cabbalistica*) and most of the Western Hermeticists mention them with different commentaries.

This is the origin of the symbols.

First, one must understand that when the observer stands anywhere in the created, everything in nature is symbolic, and that nothing is a symbol when the observer stands in the uncreated. God is reality. He sees all the forms of his work as realities. His children enjoy the same mode of perfect vision. Other men conceive as real only that corner of the universe where their spirit dwells.

Particularly in the domain of religious knowledge, which always proceeds from a revelation, symbolism exists only for the intellectuals, theorists, and speculatives. For the true mystics, who are soul-led, practical, and doers, everything is real. And from the standpoint of the "center" it is they who are right. In this particular case, one must remember the universal law of life from which so many examples have been transmitted to us by the ancient synthetic wisdoms: this law is the cross. It is the cross that gives birth, that gives life, that causes death, that transfigures. It is through the cross that beings labor, suffer, come to assume beatitude. The cross seals all things: time, space, stones, plants, biology, social life, cosmic fire; the evolution of continents, planets, ideas, religions; the movements of invisible armies, fluids, and gods. Our supreme Lord has taken it, carried it, submitted to it in his triple achievement of creator, redeemer, and enlightener.

All the visionaries transported by the spirit into the

splendid and awesome palaces where the demiurgic gods labor have seen the sign of the cross. The Atlantean sages, those of Libya, Aryavarta, of the Hundred-Families of China, those of Celtic lands and of Iran—all have described to men time and time again the splendors, the depths, the power, the harmony of the cross. If we limit our inquiry to *our* sacred books, we see that the cross fertilizes Eden, operated in the theurgic miracles of Moses, protected the magi-king; and also, that Ezekiel the prophet, crowning the ascending series of revelations, brought us, from the sacred slumber of ecstasies, the most ardent, living image of the cross prior to the arrival of the One who was to give this sign a terrestrial incarnation by the total abnegation of his human sacrifice.

The holy animals of the Jewish prophet and of the seer of Patmos are but the Egyptian sphinx on a more central plane. They represent the four universal operations of the Word—the same that the rabbinic initiates described as their four worlds, and as the tetragrammaton that all visionaries have seen (and the most simple commentaries of which are to be found in the works of Louis-Michel de Figanieres). Each gospel describes one of these operations. Each evangelist, in this way, has but written his own spiritual biography.

To teach creatures how to make use of their free will, the Father lets them walk alone. When they falter or stray, he sends them guides who lift them up or show them the right path. These are the saviors and prophets. They are more or less advanced according to the task they have to fulfill. Just as a king sends a captain, then a general to the battlefield, so the Father sent to the world soldiers, then officers, and finally the general: his Son.

The Body of the Gospels

On the one hand, prophets have had some intuition about the terrestrial future only because they possessed some recollection of a celestial past. The Messiah they were announcing—coming from a land where there is neither space nor time—could therefore not be perceived through any divining process. The prescience of prophets is a gift.

On the other hand, impelled by an imperious force to proclaim their revelations and to exhort the prince and the people to facilitate the coming of the One they had announced, their zeal often brought adversities—they suffered for their God. And is it not possible to believe that God made each of them witnesses of the realization of their hopes, in body and in spirit, according to the measure of their dedicated zeal, according to the suffering they had undergone and to the works they had accomplished? The people of the Middle Ages believed this to be true, and on a window of the Cathedral of Chartres one can see the four evangelists paired with the four great prophets. The *Hortus deliciarum* of the Abbess Herrad of Landsberg, destroyed in 1870 during the Strasbourg fire, also propounded this theory with a different illustration.

Each of these great annunciators, transported within one of the four modes of action of the Word, saw attributed to himself the sign of these modes. It would not be very difficult to prove this thesis through the esoteric study of Ezekiel, Isaiah, Daniel, and Jeremiah. And although this belongs more to kabbalistic initiation, I will explain it further.

The Word can manifest himself where, when, and how it pleases him. However, he never does anything except in view of our final happiness. As this happiness is proportionate to the power acquired by our liberty, and as this liberty is only developed by the school of obedience to a task, so the Word only appears there where his children have called him by a series of their virtuous actions. And he prepares these very acts of men (just as a schoolmaster, through loving-kindness, incites his little children to learn their lessons well) so that they may deserve the right of being rewarded.

That is why, ever since human beings appeared on earth, there has been a chosen people, whose descendants became in due time the Hebrews—a stiff-necked, uncompromising race, because the vessel in which the most active and precious balms are to be poured must be of hard stone. It was an ingrate race, because it is where the shadows are darkest that the light will burst into splendor. It was a violent and prevaricating race, because it is from the most violent poisons that the purest remedies are extracted.

A major commentary could be written on the history of Israel viewed from the mystic standpoint of the ontology of the Word. Who is the Christian kabbalist who will sign such a work?

If, looking over this panorama generally and cursorily, we consider what follows the canonical books of the Old Testament, we are immediately aware of the links in a complete system of theogony, cosmogony, and androgony. Israel was a collective unity, a plant sown after the last Deluge that grew for 4000 years in spite of catastrophes, and finally produced the perfect fruit: the Messiah. Each one of the patriarchs, kings, and Jewish prophets represents a cosmic, psychic, or terrestrial force. Each event in their history is the construction of an organ of the human personality of Christ.

The Body of the Gospels

Here I must stop. These brief indications are sufficient to fill hours of meditation. Jesus said: "I came to fulfill the law." These simple words teach us that the two Testaments complete one another as the matrix and the medal. The figure, the seed, or created sphere contained in the former are found in the second in fact, in perfection, in the Absolute. Christ comes forth before us as the Realizor par excellence.

This delineation is not of great concern to those interested only in the practical imitation of Christ: they are certain that any system is partial and biased, that for anyone not having previously mastered moral truth, intellectual truth is impossible to have, and that, after all, everything goes along as it pleases the Father that it should be. Hence, I may only give rather vague indications upon the characteristics proper to each of the gospel accounts.

Matthew's account is more complete, more practical, and the most comprehensible. It states facts, material actions, and gives to an individual his rule of conduct, to do good, and the path.

Mark's account is concise. From a certain standpoint, it gives the philosophical law; moreover, it decrees social rules: the phenomena of collective life and of objective invisible life.

Luke's account is more literary. It gives more abundant details on the Virgin and upon the judgment of the soul. It describes the sentimental, psychic, and animic worlds, beauty, and invisible subjective life.

John's account is the most mysterious and incomprehensible. Consequently it is most appreciated today. It is about the divinity of Christ and the relationship between the

Father and the Son—and about truth. It is the gospel of intellect. And were it not presumptuous to speak of the Spirit, one could call it the gospel of the Holy Spirit. St John has always been favored by the schools that the Church of Rome qualifies as heretics. Adam of Saint-Victor said that John used to pick up precious stones to give to the poor—the conclusion being that he was an alchemist. The Gnostics, Albigenses, Templars, and Waldensians venerated him, affirming that he had left an oral tradition upon which their doctrines were based. Unhappily, many of these systems were anti-Christic and purely magical—particularly a certain esotericism of the Catholic church, so often mentioned today, that is much closer to the ancient polytheistic mysteries than it is to those of the gospel.

What is this initiation of Christ? What are its characteristics, its processes and aims? It is precisely the purpose of this book to address these questions.

I do not mean to imply that the other traditions, the I-Ching, Vedas, Avesta, or Koran are false, or that their study is unnecessary. Everything has a reason for being. Each creature receives the food most assimilable for its constitution and the best for the work it has to perform. Spiritual nourishment is distributed to us with the same foresight. The I-Ching corresponds to the geometric mentality of the yellow race, which is both abstract and concrete. The Veda satisfies the love the Hindu has for rhythm and its infinite combinations, and motionless dream. Since the Old Testament is the book of an active and hard people, the gospel teaches us useful lessons of sacrifice, tolerance, and modesty. It brings down our pride as inventors and conquerors.

The Body of the Gospels

It denounces the false values of faith in money and the cult of power.

An initiation is the ensemble of methods enabling an individual to come into contact with a plane of the invisible, to acclimatize his spirit to it, to enable him to become conscious of his discoveries and acquisitions. Hence, there may be all sorts of initiations, since there are all sorts of temperaments, ideals, and invisible planes.

Some seek nothing but phenomena. Others are interested only in man. Some only see comprehensible laws. Others comprehend nothing but God. These four types are called experimenters, psychologists, metaphysicians, and mystics, respectively. Moreover, each person works from one of his centers—such as the senses, sentiments, reasoning, or intuition—to the exclusion of the others. With these simple remarks one can erect a general classification of initiations. Other keys are useful too, but among those publicly known I have never found any better tabulations than those of Hoene-Wronski in his *Messianisme*, and those of Charles Barlet in his various works. As I do not intend to give these notes a philosophical aspect, I ask the reader to refer back to the sources. He will then judge for himself if he wants to accept the following conclusions.

None of the various esotericisms and exotericisms are any closer to the truth than the other. They are refractions of the same mountain in lakes at various altitudes. Just as snow takes on a different hue according to the transparency of the water, the same azure is reflected either lighter or darker according to the color of the surfaces. Finally, all the schools belong to one of two roads. Some lead to one of the thousands of temporary paradises contained within the confines of creation. Others, starting from all planes of creation, fuse into the one narrow, unique, and direct path leading to the Absolute. In the Light, human spirits are automatically classified depending on whether they believe in gods, in themselves, or in God.

All searchers have heard of mysterious fraternities and unknown adepts living in the wilderness. That such men exist, I do not doubt. Those who have quenched their thirst at Asiatic springs consider themselves superior to those in the shadow of the Pyramid. But then again, these latter, who manifest themselves under the title of Rosicrucians, consider the Eastern doctrines corrupt. Since I am writing about the gospels, it would be ill-fitting for me to express contempt towards these admirable men and for their superhuman wisdom. In any event, initiatory states remain incomprehensible to the common crowd. No one knows what differentiates a Pháp from an Arhat or Jivanmukti, an Abdai from a Bhakta, unless one has been all of these. Whoever claims an adept's title proves thereby that he does not possess it.

We must state here and now (as the following pages will verify) that the Eastern wisdoms: Chinese, Hindu, and Muslim, are all anti-Christic. In neither Damas, Lhassa, or Benares—in no crypt, desert, or mountain of Asia—does any initiate recognize Christ as God by birth, as identical with God.

Only the true Rosicrucians have adopted this axiom. But so many demi-adepts have usurped this title, that it should first be defined. In any case, since 1680 they have changed names, so that all who have since then boasted being such have only proven themselves braggarts. And as for today, who has not heard something or other about pseudo-Rosicrucians?

The Body of the Gospels

Let us leave these puerilities aside! The Counsellor von Eckartshausen has enumerated the most likely characteristics of the state of the Rosicrucian soul in his little book *The Cloud Over the Sanctuary*, as has also Lopoukine in his *A Few Aspects of the Inner Church*. In truth, the first book of *The Imitation of Christ* of Thomas à Kempis gives the finest method of attaining that state which one can describe but superficially as an unstable equilibrium between matter and spirit. It is a communication between one of the palaces of the Word and the earth; it is a series of contacts and of interruptions between the spirit of man and the spirit of the Word. Dr. Marc Haven says that Solomon's *Song of Songs* is the book that most thoroughly describes this function, and that each newborn brother of the Rosicrucians, upon entering the order, must furnish an original commentary of this book. The Association is not concerned only about one's individual asceticism. Rather, it pursues all means by which social harmony, international peace, a universal republic, religious unity, and concord between experimental science, reasoning philosophy, and intuitive faith can be achieved. It has an immense function worthy of all our respect and of our efforts in its behalf.

⊕

However, it constitutes but one of the initiatory modes comprised in the teaching of the gospels. No one has yet encompassed the spiritual horizon of these four divine accounts. No other book contains an equal sum of knowledge. No revelation more complete has ever been offered to any creature on earth or on any other planet, visible or invisible. And if the least among men would read one verse of the gospel each morning and make it his own in his daily life—then, come what may, he would reach the eternal city in a few days, and the moment would soon come when the earth, not being able to withstand the splendid conflagration of that heart, would send him back to that kingdom from which we are exiled.

No science is needed to understand the words of Christ. His secret is both open and hidden. It is crystal-clear for the hearts who live in the kingdom, but to others it is as undecipherable as the most obscure hieroglyphics of ancient sages. Patient study of the old texts may reveal three, seven, fifty, or one-hundred-and-eight interpretations (we are familiar with the rules of such esoteric cryptography)—but the mysteries contained in the gospel keep well hidden because they belong to the Spirit. It is the Holy Spirit alone that reveals them to us, in proportion to our submission. Gospel phraseology in the "comprehensible" sphere contains simultaneously a fact, a sentiment, and an idea amalgamated through a spiritual perception of the heart—which is nothing else than the presence of an angel from the Word, because all that our Jesus has thought, felt, and done is alive forever.

In any event, the goal of our life is not taking cognizance of arcana. No matter under what pompous term we may want to designate it, it would still be but satisfying our curiosity. The gospel asks only that day by day we abandon ourselves to the Father as therein contained, making of it the necessary element of our life. Since the Father knows all our needs, if he has not given us the necessary faculties that permit us to master foreign tongues, perform kabbalistic calculations on the science of letters, or work out subtle analogies on the value of words—in short, if he has not placed teachers, visible or invisible, on our path to teach us

The Body of the Gospels

these things—it is because they are of no use to the perfecting of our life at this time. Later we will consider the methods of true intellectual hygiene. But exegesis and the science of hieroglyphics are not necessary for this. The simple man who lives and puts into practice the little he has understood will find more truths in a second-rate version than the erudite, who, compiling notes and comparing manuscripts, will ever discover in the most authentic texts.

Each being receives his proper food. Individuals, races, and worlds are fed in the material, the etheric, and the spiritual planes with matter, ethers, or spirits borrowed from the milieu in which they dwell. These three planes are always connected with one another, just as the lymphatic canals, arteries, and nerves connect the organs of alimentation, respiration, sensation, and motion. Some objective beings exist whose function is to make material life, etheric life, and spiritual life communicate. A book is one of these beings.

In principle, man possesses within himself the seeds of all knowledge and powers. The fact is, however, that he smothers most of these seeds; and books are one of the regenerating rays that passes through intelligence. One may also be initiated by feeling or sentiment (that lies within the province of the psychurgist). But perfect initiation is not the book, slumber in a crypt, or magical experiences. It does not go from below to above, or from outer to inner. On the contrary, it bursts open in the spiritual heart, and from there propagates itself in all the other organisms of man. Christ alone illumines in that way. Any other master, even a god, has influence only upon the sheath of the heart.

Ontologically speaking, man should develop only from

the center to the circumference. But he has become corrupted—has fallen ill. Heaven sends him healers. These are the awakeners, and their chief is Christ. But we do not understand this Healer. Some (Dupuis) see him as an astronomical symbol. Vaillant sees him as a solar myth, a legendary figure, an agitator. Others, who know a little esotericism, take him for a magnetist, a medium, or a magician. The Muslims, Babists, occultists, pantheists, Theosophists, and Orientals affirm that he was a student of the Essenes or of the Brahmans, that he purloined the incommunicable Name, or that he was an unfledged Buddha.

Let us realize that Christ is the Son of God, and God himself—accepting the full and literal meaning with which these words are endowed. He had nothing to learn from anyone, because he knew all things. He did not need to follow any training, because he could do all things, even from the time of his birth.

Nonetheless, I can understand why so many fallacies have been spoken about him: the being who brings a new torch lit from the divine hearth incarnates and realizes the biological law of the place to which he descends. Calendars and liturgical years have been erected upon the events of his terrestrial life, such as has been done for Ram, Osiris, and Krishna.

Jesus is the ideal, the model of relative perfection. Within his life, the alchemist will discover the philosopher's stone, and the magician will find the formula for his arcana. Christ, the perfect model as Savior, has the right and the power to use all of nature's forces. Hence, each school may claim him as theirs, since each initiate sees him according to the lenses he fabricated for himself during his initiation. Christ is a man. He is also a universal law. Moreover, he is

The Body of the Gospels

God. What is incomprehensible is how all those illusionary aspects are conciliated, unified, and transfigured into the inexpressible reality he reveals only to the poor in spirit.

⊕

How should the gospel be read? How should one attempt to find the infinite horizons hidden within such simple sentences? How is anyone able to follow the infinite and immeasurable prolongations of divine thought?

Here are three keys among hundreds. May those who have just emerged from the labyrinth of occult sciences use them. We will then see how those who advance along the path of intellectual poverty proceed.

All pursuits of knowledge are classified under three headings: God, man, and universe. They are perceptible by the senses, by feeling, by the intellect, or by intuition. Such is the framework. And each order of science must be utilized by a corresponding practical art.

Hence, the chart below.

object	universe	man	God
the senses	natural sciences, physico-chemistry-mathematics	physiology ethnology language	cosmogonies mythologies morality
intellect	astronomy geology signatures etc.	psychology sociology history esthetics	theology metaphysics religion
intuition	occult sciences alchemy, numbers	symbolism psychurgy Initiation	mysticism theurgy regeneration

This is merely the outline of a classification. Each student may develop other models from it (better ones, doubtless, since he will have found them himself).

THE CHILDHOOD OF JESUS

Here are other methods:

The exegetic angles that have brought renown to Fr Richard Simon, Krauss, Renan, Reithmeyer, Muratori, Ernest Havet, Reville, Heulhard, the Abbé Loisy, and many others (in order to mention all opinions) interest us only as curiosities. It is all external. And as we have already said, the gematria calculations of Hebrew, Greek, or Latin texts are also nothing but intellectual methods.

Each account may be studied as describing a particular aspect of the Word: objectively or subjectively. To be more concise, the following chart will explain our meaning better.

Matthew	*Mark*	*Luke*	*John*
Man	Lion	Ox	Eagle
androgyny	invisible nature	visible nature	God
ethology	environments	the three kingdoms	the three Persons
sociology	spirits	natural sciences, etc.	way, truth, life
study of man under all aspects, morality, etc., the process of this study can be:	elementals the gods pneumatology astrology		three witnesses: water, blood & spirit (1st Epistle of John) mystical union, etc.
philosophical	analogical	naturalistic	metaphysical
didactic	aesthetic	sensorial	religious
meditative	by sentiment	facts	intuitional
reasoning	inspiration	observation	ecstasy
intuitive	beauty	goodness	the inexpressible

It is quite interesting to consider the four gospels together in order to find out:

The historical Christ as redeemer
The psychic Christ as regenerator
The cosmic Christ as creator

The Body of the Gospels

But in order to follow didactic methods, or any others we might invent, one should have a complete and thorough knowledge of the subject. I do not possess it. I will then hold to the conviction that human methods of knowledge are limited. And so we will read together a synoptic gospel, and I will acquaint you during the reading with the results I believe myself to have obtained, and those I remember.

As soon as the vibrations of the words uttered by the Word touched our planet's atmosphere two thousand years ago, they received faithful guardians. Ambition, political tyranny, greed, or spiritual pride have been kept from altering their actual sense. The gospel is the description of life in the center, in the heart, and in the sanguine system of the universe.

	Matthew	*Mark*	*Luke*	*John*
figures	man/angel	lion	ox	eagle
country of destination	Jews	Romans Arabs	Phoenicians Syrians	Alexandrians Greeks
zodiacal signs	aquarius	leo	taurus	scorpio
tarots	cups	swords	coins	rods
elements	water or earth	fire	earth or water	air
cardinal points	west	south or north	north or south	east
tetragram	2nd hé	vau	hé	iod
theology	Messiah	Father	Son	Holy Spirit
kabbalah	metatron shekinah	Ancient One	Matron	Holy Breath
sephiroth	malkuth	kether	hochmah	binah
patriarchs	Jacob	Juda	Abraham	Isaac

THE CHILDHOOD OF JESUS

prophets	Isaiah	Daniel	Jeremiah	Ezekiel
prophets	Isaiah	Ezekiel	Daniel	Jeremiah
their public	followers	leaders	animics (who follow their hearts)	intellectuals
objects	the Way the Good	external life (invisible)	subjective life (beauty)	truth verity

The type of symbolism used in the parables indicate to us that the physical plane is the most important manifestations for man of life on earth, and the most fruitful for his future. It is in this direction that we have the most direct relation with the heart of the world and with the Word. Based upon that fact, wishful thinking is nil, while our actions have paramount importance. We must not become disinterested in our family, society, country, or profession. We are far better off living our prosaic existence than choosing the ivory tower of the philosopher or the solitude of the ascetic. That is the conclusion I hope my readers will reach after having read this book.

The Gospel in the Invisible World

Simplicity—What is the gospel?—Its biological principle—Its reason for being—What is a book?—Speech—Words—Names—Of which invisible plane is the gospel the embodiment?—Why was it given to us?—How to read it—Summary

UR CURIOSITY disregards the greatest miracles. It does not even notice them, perhaps because God multiplies them around us. While the whole landscape unfolds its wealth and its enchantments, we hypnotize ourselves over a stone. We do not really know how to see, because we look with worry and haste. How many marvels could be unveiled, were we willing to listen to the silent affirmation that attests the existence of God within us, and his untiring tenderness! First of all, we must return to simplicity, throw off the clinging tentacles of artificiality, and admit to ourselves that we are not much. Why do we not jump into the refreshing waves of the source of life?

Interrogate the silence of your heart. Do so because you know there exists an eternal fountain of strength, light, and peace; that from it inexhaustible streams spread throughout invisible fields; and that there is not a path devoid of the murmur of its regenerating waters. All we need do is shed our garments—these artificial cloaks we think we should wear when we go in search of the thousand faces of truth.

THE CHILDHOOD OF JESUS

If you are searching for religious truths, shake off exegesis. It is a cumbersome cloak. Throw away the superfluous ornaments of apologetics. Get rid of hermeneutics and dogmatism. Forget patristics for a while. But especially, let go the ambiguous mysterious sciences exhumed out of polytheistic wisdom.

Aim for simplicity. From a negative virtue, let it become the active, forceful virtue of simpleness. Plunge your whole heart into the cool fountain of love, and a veil will be lifted from your eyes. Nature will appear to you as innocent and magnificent, because your eyes will be without guile. The infinite perspectives of existence will never cause you to become discouraged anymore.

Then take a book in your hands. The life contained therein will communicate itself to the life within you. The material life of this volume will speak to the life of your fingers, of your eyes, of your lips. The paper and the characters are merely actors in physico-chemical and etheric dramas. They are faithful registrars who carry the image of all beings who have handled them, of all scenes to which they were witness, of studio or room and furniture through which they passed. They are still palpitating from the work of the overseers. Above all, within them the very life of the author has been voluntarily imprisoned, has been incarnated with all it possesses of personal and immortal wealth and idealism.

You readers, you satisfy a desire either for entertainment, for study, for your enthusiasm, or to be appeased. What are desires if not the primitive forms of life, or radical needs for the expansion and unfolding of the self? And what gives the self the strength to seek perfection except feeling its own inadequacies by tacit comparison with its ideal?

The Gospel in the Invisible World

Reading is the search for one's ideal by means of the ideal of another. It is the union of two ideals and of all their mental, esthetic, and even physical expressions. For example, the hand that turns the pages modifies the state of the paper. And at the contact of the paper, the life of our fingers is modified. Force is poured from our eyes unto the printed letters, just as these letters influence the life of our retina. Our intellect voices ideas of which these words are the bodies. Finally, in the august silence of eternal space our soul commences ineffable colloquies with the souls of those ideas fixed upon the pages.

To read is a drama, because each form contains an aspect of the absolute. What profound efforts from the reader! See how thirsty he is for knowledge, how anxious he is to understand, how he tries, how he hastens, how painfully he stumbles—but how he takes flight anyway! What joy he feels when he has been able to grasp the scintillating robe of the idea!

Yet, that idea is not hostile to man. It loves him and wants to live with him. It is we who are clumsy. It is our selfish covetousness that erects thorny hedges between the angels of intelligence and ourselves. These emissaries also become bruised and extenuated on the uneven pathways of terrestrial thought.

We would be amazed and abashed with regrets if all of a sudden our eyes would open and were able to see how many beings work and labor to enable a schoolboy to understand Plato or Kant. Nothing takes place without the collaboration of a host of workmen. Between the student and his book there come and go elemental spirits, angels, spirits of past readers, the image of all the actions incited by that particular book, and even the soul of the author—that enthusiastic and grave martyr who once upon a time knew how to give his life in order to offer that Idea the indispensable body for its terrestrial mission. What a waste it is when we read merely to "kill time" or to encourage our wrongdoing! What responsibility!

⊕

What then is a *book*? There again is another and more painful drama. It is a weighty mission: that of bringing to men the reflection of immortal kingdoms. The writer and the artist fulfill a sacerdotal function. Look at the heart of those who fulfill their solemn task, of those whom neither fortune nor honors can swerve from their contemplation. Thinkers consider themselves indebted to humanity for the august joys they experience in their contacts with their goddesses. See how prestige crowns their brow. They radiate calm, though raging storms may at times be devastating their own inner fields. Their spirits suffer from perpetual gestation. They feel themselves unworthy to receive the genii of Beauty or the gods of Truth. They grieve at not being able to report the dialogues of invisible beings with sufficient fire. They accept the most precarious, saddest, existence because they know that each suffering undergone, each pain borne, is another brush stroke on the canvas they are painting of their own secret visitations.

A *work* is the most difficult evocation. No magus in the crypts of Ancient Memphis has ever attempted any as painful, especially none as fecund in seeds of light.

Yet no creature creates. Man himself can only reproduce in time and space some of the marvels his soul remembers having perceived in eternity and in infinity.

Does his soul remember? No, it perceives. It perceives

because the soul is just as much a part of that eternal, and of that infinite, as was the first grain of wheat that, brought on earth a long time ago, contained the billions of sheaths we are even now harvesting.

In the Kingdom, the Son is the concept or the idea of the Father, which expresses itself through a free, living, and individual form, by a being. In nature, on the contrary, forms participate in the inertia, the amorphous, and the fatality of the void. The incessantly gushing and various expressions of divine will people the kingdom. Their shadows people this universe. They register at their departure, at the end of the errand, and at their return. This triple census produces three books that are but one: the Book of Life. Thus are set the providential decrees, the activity of creatures and of future events, offspring of the contacts between God's will and human wills. These eternal archives project the triple conception of number, sign, and name upon human intellect.

It is because an earth soul was able to remember having seen the eternal book (perused by the luminous hands of angels) in the magnificent perspectives of the house of the Father, that it was able to set down the memory of important events by a more durable sign than a gesture or a cry.

A creature possesses three great faculties: movement, reproduction, and expression. Inner movements are expressed by gestures, by mimicry, by the voice, and handwriting, just as the shape of the body denotes the static constitution of the spirit.

All the atoms of the Absolute, if I may use such an improper term, are angels. When the Father sends them into temporal space, each of these pure seeds expresses itself by molding matter according to the divine quality it possesses. Nothing exists save that the Father wanted it so. Sounds, colors, densities, laws of physics, and thought do not exist of necessity. The Father could have constituted his creation in an entirely different manner—there can be an infinity of other ontological modes. These modes will always remain inconceivable to us because we can only imagine them by means of elements borrowed from the very nature of which we are merely parts.

Thus, a book is an idea only in the world of ideas, just as it is a thing in the world of things. We make use of it without understanding it any more than we understand other objects. It is an ensemble of signs. It is the outward expression of inner dramas. But it fulfills this function only because the decisions and projects of the Father and their results are registered in the kingdom.

It seems to me unnecessary to erect a theory of signs, to classify their various states or dynamics, their forms or motions, their articulate or inarticulate sounds, or the gestures projected by handwriting. To explain philology and hieroglyphics is but describing approximate appearances. It is not possible to conceive how the invisible becomes visible, the abstract concrete, the idea a word, force a form. The fundamental axioms of geometry and of arithmetic, though they may seem self-evident, are nothing but axioms of faith: we use them without understanding them. Let us ask, rather: what is form? what is a number?

No one has given a true answer to these questions since the world began. The very ancient teachers of the science of signatures or qualitative geometry, of the science of numbers or qualitative mathematics, have really transmitted to

The Gospel in the Invisible World

us only empirical data. What do their aphorisms convey to our intellect? Say: "Letters are alive." But what does that mean? The most learned esotericists see nothing but symbols within these axioms.

Yet they are not symbols. In the world from which the gospel came, that which our brain calls 4, 10, 1000, a square, a pyramid, or a parabola, are living individualities. Our brain has two eyes on the physical plane, but it also has a quantity of invisible pairs of eyes. We are conscious only of the least fraction of these organs, and do not perceive them under their true form. Rather, our psycho-physical faculties, such as memory, judgment, comparison, abstraction, enumeration, esthetics, etc., refract them to us. Many of these eyes are only in a seed stage, so that at this time we are only able to see a few of these worlds beyond the material one. When we will have become perfect, we will have an eye for each of the countless planes that constitute the totality of the cosmos. But for now we do not know these fractions of the universe as they are. Between them and our eyes is a milieu that deforms. And in any case, our eye itself does not register the image integrally. To see perfectly, one should have a perfect organ able to annul the influence of the milieu. Also, as the perfection of a flower depends upon the perfect health of the root, so, in order to know truth, one must have a pure heart.

That is why the perfect man, the free man, instantly knows the truth about anything. The spirit that is in him permits him to have the subject he is interested in present before him—either because he may transport himself to it by an inner act, or because he may have the subject appear before him at will. Such is the omniscience of Christ, which we too will receive someday.

THE CHILDHOOD OF JESUS

⊕

It can be said that name, expression, and relation coexist in the Absolute as three persons of a trinity signifying the divine Trinity. Each being created by the Father receives a distinctive sign: his *name*, a distinctive *form* (his own word, quality of life, or his function), and a place that links him to the other children of the Father (his order or *number*, if I may use such a prosaic expression).

These three signs of creative power are equal, simultaneous, consubstantial. Their shadow engenders in the world the ensemble of all intellectual faculties among men, and also among those beyond men.

One can understand the motive that led the hierophants to baptize their disciples with a new name after their initiation, to impose particular functions upon them, and to furnish them with a numerical key. Baptism, which is part of all societies and of almost all religions, is not a ceremony peculiar to this planet. Each time a creature enters a new mansion, he is given a new name. And the choice of names, as the future will prove, is never left to chance. Parents believe they are free to choose their children's names: they are not aware of being bound.

In practical occultism, as well as in all initiations, as you know, names play an important part. Sorcerers often have to know and to pronounce the name of their victims exactly. The Brahmans consider the science of sounds (*laya vidya, laya yoga*) and the science of incantations (*mantra*) as very powerful. Religions make use of it: witness the Buddhist, Christian, and Muslim rosaries, and the litanies.

When we invoke a saint, we call him by name. When we pray for someone, we name him.

The Father watches over each of us by means of an angel

The Gospel in the Invisible World

who is the living realization of his solicitude. That angel needs a sign to designate the men under his care. That sign is their name. But he alone who knows and possesses pure spirit may know the eternal name.

Above the material worlds ("above" meaning "within"), above the etheric worlds that astrologers study, beyond the empyrean where forms, diagrams, schemas, and yantras emit luminous rays, is to be found the world of numbers. This arithmology is incomprehensible especially to we of earth because this planet was particularly given speech. The adepts' speculations on mathematics barely represents the alpha-beta of the true science of numbers, though they think they possess it. Finally (and still above all of this) is found the world of eternal names. Such is the vestibule of the library in the Father's house.

⊕

Let us try to obtain a precise idea from the varied meanings that it is possible to extract from the sacred texts.

As with any intellectual or aesthetic work, or any work from human genius, these venerable books explain inner truths that are from beyond the terrestrial, and at times even from beyond the supernatural. A writer does not invent. He copies a being or an inner, invisible, or abstract spectacle. He traces either an exact or a beautiful image according to the depth of his union with that being, and according to his talent for expression. The reader in turn communicates with this being by means of the book in proportion to his attention, intellectual humility, and enthusiasm—or, as we might say, according to the recognition he has of his ignorance, to the absence of preconceived ideas, and to the invisible world where his spirit resides.

Hence, each reader forms an entirely different conception of the same book. The ancient sages even tried to systematize this multiplicity of concepts by establishing a framework beforehand. You know their theory.

They classified the manifestations of universal life, giving a significant name to each compartment either by form or by sound. From these simple signs they formed alphabets, words, then idioms. These sacred tongues are not identical: they each differ according to the spiritual summit reached by the initiatory school that conceived them.

One such school divided the world, or the knowledge of the world, into 22 titles, another divided it into 25; others into 23, 50, 64, and even 108. The disciple is warned that each word of the text may be applied to each of the worlds as enumerated by his school. That is why each sacred book simultaneously covers history, physical sciences, physiology, sociology, magic, cosmology, etc., according to the number of compartments of the system adopted.

The mystagogues were more or less conscious visionaries. Their particular gods (say, Osiris, Adonai, Brahma, and Ahura-Mazdao) transported each of them to the summit of their respective kingdoms, from where they were able to acquire a general knowledge of the cosmos. This was so, because it is understood that the adept speaks only of the mysteries he personally has been able to contact in his ecstasies. But these explorations, no matter how difficult or meritorious they may be, are only equal to the knowledge of the Alpine climber who observes the topography of the countryside, the importance of the villages, forests, waterways, and cultivation—but who does not really experience the manners, customs, and habits proper to the inhabitants of the region. Thus, the revelatory religious visionaries

The Gospel in the Invisible World

described what they had seen by means of a Logosophy inspired by their own gods.

Since all is contained in the All, each system contains some aspect of supreme truth. No created being is deprived of the inner intuition of this truth. In itself, it is the law of heaven, the will of the Father. And simultaneously it is the reality of creation and the biological rule of creatures, since the environments are organized for their inhabitants and the inhabitants for their environments.

This universal organon is the "Word." When Christ says "I am the way, the truth, the life," one must understand that the "way" is the rule of action, the "truth" is the ideal or aim, and the "life" is the means of attaining it.

Hence, it is to those who accept the supra-intellectual fact of the divinity of Christ, only Son of God, and God himself (and to those alone) that I address myself, for they will understand that the gospel is the unedited and authentic extract of the Law of Laws, that in spite of all the maneuvers of the Adversary and adulterations due to human vices, nothing essential has been erased. And finally, because these stories came from the living center of truth they possess the unique power of being self-expressive, of being adaptable to the intellect of anyone so as to extend, condense, enlighten, or overshadow their horizons—as if there were an angel standing in the atmosphere before the reader regulating the flow of light according to the capacity of the human eyes open upon it. Such is the secret, the hieroglyphics, the anagogy of the gospels.

⊕

If you believe that Jesus is God, you will conceive that his acts and his works surpass earthly limits, that their radiation reaches universal auditors, that their influence overflows from the vessel of planetary time. His acts and works live off the very life of their Author. They are, strictly speaking, angels of this Word who engenders and pronounces them perpetually.

So, do not dissect the gospels according to ternary, septenary, or denary formulas. Do not try to scout out 22, 52, or any other number of meanings. The gospels contain all the meanings, or rather, one meaning only: the true one, the meaning of the center from which they emanate.

Do not read them solely with your intelligence, else you will not perceive life in them. Do not make use only of your acquired knowledge, else you will only limit your instruction. Your intelligence and your knowledge are partial. Study these books with the supra-intellect of your being—with your heart. Comprehension will come later. Better yet, when you read the gospel, recall to mind that heaven penetrates all things, that the Christic notion of the Absolute is not that of a separate domain, but of an essence (a vital mode contained in the bosom of all relative existences), that unity is the world of synthetic union and not that of analytical isolation. If you do this, you will read the gospel and interrogate it with your entire being. It is written: "You will love God with all thy heart, with all thy soul, all thy mind, and all thy strength."

Christ's words nourish our heart, our reason, our philosophical needs, our esthetic sensitivity, our subtle currents, even our body. Were the material and semi-material organisms willing, they too would receive forces (certain disciples have proven the point). However, in order to enter into the kingdom of unity, to live in it, one must have built unity within oneself beforehand.

The Gospel in the Invisible World

Yet, we find but two fundamental or vital modes in the universe. The one that we *experience* is diversity. The one that we *crave* is unity. We can enter into the latter only by abandoning the former. Let not the body seek to satisfy its desire anymore; let the "double" renounce its pleasures; let the astral body and the mental body and all others renounce their joy. May all of them seek no further but to grasp the light while living the life of life: the law. These are the means by which the individual will know his ignorance, how his personality will become simple, and how the self, becoming aware of the magnificent horizons, will become able to move through them as the legitimate heir of divine-lordship.

Man's natural life is exalted by death, and propagates itself by fragmentation; it is not really living: this incessant battle against nothingness is an effort towards life.

Divine life is a ceaseless outpouring, a plenitude without interstices, an eternal present, a generation without struggles, a stable ubiquity, a motion devoid of obstacles, a pacific harmony. Because God is the Living One, the words of his Son live: they are beings, they are angels. When Jesus cures the blind, it is an angel who comes on earth and remains here at the disposal of all the blind people who are able to recognize the special halo of these messengers. When Jesus speaks of the lily, of the fig tree, of the lame, of the prodigal son, or of anything else, these again are angels who descend to live in the interior of the terrestrial space assigned to those who suffer, to plants, to joys, to repentance.

These angels answer the calls sent towards their Lord. Our aspirations for the light give them the means of helping us. For them we open the door of the secret garden.

They procure for us purification, illumination, and power. They modify our future: unbeknown to us, in hasty conventicles, they agree to coordinate our modest efforts. They give us the indications of how to decorate the chamber of honor where, some stormy night, we will lodge the eternal Pilgrim—their Lord and Friend.

⊕

Please try to understand how the gospel gives strength to those who consult it with confidence. I do not mind repeating that it is a living book. We are so overcome by the suffocating of the valley of death that we cannot conceive now life shines elsewhere. The gospel contains a blessing: the fingers that turn the pages, the eyes that read, the ears that listen, the paper of which the volume is composed, and also the type—all these receive from its angel this silent blessing, the most powerful blessing, because of him from whom these pages come.

How shall we receive it? We, the creatures far superior to paper, ink, and metal, and yet—just because of our superiority—that much the more responsible? How shall we receive this non-human, non-systematic truth, this buoyant and free light suited to our actual and personal state, and that suits the state of all those bound to us?

If the reader has reached the gospel only after having fallen into all chasms of pain, only after having extracted the disenchanted essence of the tree of knowledge, after having sucked human sentiments dry; if he reaches this source naked and hungry, tired and bruised; if his obstinate hope has no more strength but that of beseeching—then he needs no other preparations in order to drink long draughts of the light gushing from this mystical rock.

The Gospel in the Invisible World

Neither does the ordinary student need to have recourse to the occult processes of investigation. He knows that the foremost obstacles to the development of intelligence are owing first of all to a lack of profound application, then to the false certitude and pride he has of his own acquisition, and finally to his intention of keeping all he learns from this science for his own welfare. Hence, he must concentrate his intellect and extend his heart. He must place himself face to face before God in total adoration. He must forget his worries, no matter whence they spring. He must plunge himself into the kindness of the Father with the confidence and feeling that all is well. Let him measure his ignorance, that he may become convinced of his littleness, of his poverty, since no one possesses anything that is not a gift from above.

He must become aware that his Friend is ever by his side, ever ready to instruct, sustain, and help him. Before the spectacle of this immense and immutable tenderness, he must then face himself—his selfishness and his laziness—so that, considering all the good he neglected doing and the help he disdained, he might repent. Repentance is indispensable. It is the harrow that tills the soul.

Only then might he present himself again before the Father to do him homage and offer himself, from his bone-marrow to the summit of his spirit, since all these working instruments come from God.

Finally, after having asked that error be take away from him, the disciple begins his studies. And when he has finished, if he has not received any new ideas, let him offer thanks for the patience that developed in him. If he has learned something, let him still be thankful. It is always advantageous to succinctly note the results obtained.

THE CHILDHOOD OF JESUS

A while back I stated that it is not necessary to employ esoteric methods for meditation—yet I have just indicated twelve or thirteen points from one of them. Esotericism calls forth forces that man has not yet the right of using. While these meticulous prescriptions are executed through the affective centers, it is the heart that prostrates itself, repents, and becomes enthused. We also have the right of disposing of our love. Moreover, prudence is essential when we take our first steps upon the mystical path: we must establish solid bases within us. Let us take many precautions. Those who have received from heaven a direct and concise "sign," and who in the Invisible wear the uniform of "soldier"—those may forego prudence: all they have to do is march. But such men are rare. And even this function is but another step towards the new birth—towards the baptism of the Spirit.

⊕

Let us recapitulate. The "words" by which the world was formed are fragments of divine life, and they animate this universe too. The sages have given to them the name of the "Word." In them the development of creatures is contained. They are their biological laws.

When the Word took a terrestrial form, he pronounced the words proper to this earth. He vivified them and explained them by his actions. The gospel contains the essential part of these lights. All the other religious codes that appeared before and after him contain only the shadow of the Christic lights that were projected by the spiritual collectives of the various races.

In the gospel one finds the practical synopses of that segment of supreme truth that each of all sciences, philosophies, religions, and initiations possess in part. Its treasures are boundless, inexhaustible. For the past twenty centuries we have inventoried but a thousandth part of it.

In this universe there exist resplendent creatures before whose beauty, intelligence, and power our imagination would be numbed, were we even able to imagine them. The very rarefied air next to these prestigious geniuses would be deadly to us, and the halo of the energies they radiate would immediately shatter our wan organisms. Yet these cherubim who handle thunder and these seraphim with the nimbus of splendid intellect do not possess in their paradisiacal sojourns lights any deeper than those contained in the one humble little volume of the New Testament, which is their hearth. However: they know and appreciate the value of this jewel more than we do.

And so, no matter how precarious our life may seem, however desolate our weaknesses or uncertainties, we are not disinherited. Let us remember that the solicitude of the Father, the tenderness of the Son, and the help of the Holy Spirit go first to the meek, to those who feel weak but who work as if they were strong.

To be nothing in ourselves, to be all in God: that is the secret of eternal life. This is all explained in the divine pages that we will read together. I sincerely hope that we find therein torches to enlighten the darkness, manna for our weakness, remedies for all ills, and an ineffable Presence in our solitude.

The Genealogy of Jesus

HIS IS THE GENEALOGY of Jesus the Messiah the son of David, the son of Abraham: Abraham was the father of Isaac, Isaac was the father of Jacob, Jacob was the father of Judah and his brothers, Judah begat Phares and Zara of Thamar; Phares begat Esrom; and Esrom begat Aram. Aram begat Aminadab; Aminadab begat Naasson and Naasson begat Salmon; Salmon begat Booz of Rachab; Booz begat Obed of Ruth; and Obed begat Jesse; Jesse begat David the king: David the king begat Solomon of her that had been the wife of Urias; Solomon begat Roboam, Roboam begat Abia; Abia begat Asa; Asa begat Josaphat; Josaphat begat Joram; Joram begat Ozias; Ozias begat Joatham; Joatham begat Achaz; Achaz begat Ezekias; Ezekias begat Manasses; Manasses begat Amon; Amon begat Josias; Josias begat Jechonias and his brethren about the time they were carried away to Babylon; after they were brought to Babylon, Jechonias begat Salathiel; Salathiel begat Zorobabel; Zorobabel begat Abiud; Abiud begat Eliakim; Eliakim begat Azor; Azor begat Zadoc and Zadoc begat Achim; Achim begat Eliud; Eliud begat Eleazar; Eleazar begat Matthan; Matthan begat Jacob. And Jacob begat Joseph the husband of Mary, of whom was born Jesus, who is called CHRIST—so all

The Genealogy of Jesus

the generations from Abraham to David are fourteen generations; and from David until the carrying away into Babylon are fourteen generations, and from the carrying away into Babylon unto Christ are fourteen generations. (Matthew 1:1–17)

And Jesus ... was the son of Joseph who was the son of Heli, son of Matthat, son of Levi, son of Melchi, son of Janna, son of Joseph, son of Mattathias, son of Amos, son of Naum, son of Esli, son of Nagge, son of Mahath, son of Mattathias, son of Semei, son of Joseph, son of Judah, son of Joanna, son of Rhesa, son of Zorobabel, son of Salathiel, son of Neri, son of Melchi, son of Addi, son of Cosam, son of Elmodam, son of Er, son of Jose, son of Eliezer, son of Jorim, son of Matthat, son of Levi, son of Simeon, son of Judah, son of Joseph, son of Jonan, son of Eliakim, son of Melea, son of Menan, son of Mattatha, son of Nathan, son of David, son of Jesse, son of Obed, son of Boaz, son of Salmon, son of Naasson, son of Aminadab, son of Aram, son of Esrom, son of Thares, son of Judah, son of Jacob, son of Isaac, son of Abraham, son of Thara, son of Nachor, son of Sarug, son of Ragau, son of Phaleg, son of Heber, son of Sala, son of Cainan, son of Arphaxad, son of Shem, son of Noah, son of Lamech, son of Mathusala, son of Enoch, son of Jared, son of Maleleel, son of Cainan, son of Enos, son of Seth the son of Adam who was created by God. (Luke 3:23–38)

The Messiah sums up the organic laws of the world. From the first page of gospel concordances, one sees at his feet the union of two currents frothing with effort, two currents of hopes, of waiting, of sacrifices, and of prayers: these are the

THE CHILDHOOD OF JESUS

precursors. One ascends from the earth; history describes its march. The other descends from heaven: the angels alone, in a whisper, tell us of the marvelous adventures of its voyage. The first is the dual genealogy of Luke and of Matthew; the second is John the Baptist. Thus it is that any flower, any star, any beauty, may unfold only by the conjunction of an evolutive or involutive force. In that incontestable law let us discern the universal figure of the cross.

Why did the scrupulous publican and the lettered doctor take the trouble to copy these precise and mysterious lists, doubtless from the public tablets in the Temple? Matthew begins only with Abraham and descends to Joseph through forty-two generations. Luke on the contrary goes back from Joseph to the first man, counting seventy-seven generations, enumerating twenty-one generations from Abraham to Adam.

Six times, eleven times, three times seven: the mysterious multiples of a number that expresses the providential law of our planet, an incomprehensible progression where the Christ appears. Where is the superhuman brain who will explain this to you? Where is the living science of numbers to be found, since none of the sages who think they possess it are able to create a living work by numbers? Let us not presume, and after having read the first page of the gospel, let us have the courage to humbly admit our ignorance. Jesus was the first to glorify inner poverty.[1]

---

[1] As stated in the preceding chapter, the paraphernalia of all sciences will be left aside in this book. The esotericist must not be surprised at not finding any parallels with theogonies, cosmogonies, or ancient initiations; nor to learn that Abraham represents the etheric space between heaven and earth; that David (whose name is significant) in Numbers has the number 14: "the noun, the son"; that the initials of Abraham, of

The Genealogy of Jesus

It has been said that Matthew names the actual fathers, and Luke names the legal fathers—a not unlikely distinction due to the Levirate customs. Others affirm that Matthew follows the rights of succession to the throne, while Luke follows the real descent. Cornelius à Lapide believes the two lists give the ancestors of the Virgin only: Matthew on the maternal side, Luke on the paternal. Modernists believe that Matthew establishes the descent of Joseph, while Luke establishes the ascent of Mary. To one critic, these are insoluble questions. We will not examine them, neither will we undertake the study of the hieroglyphs included in the one hundred and twenty names. We have interdicted our entering into the domain of esotericism. It would limit us. Let us not build any more systems.

Let us liberate ourselves.[2] In our times, we have need not so much for science as for supernatural forces. Let us scale these summits that the men in the valley hardly know exist. Let us soar towards the superhuman heavens that the sublime ignorance of faith alone travels.

If each biblical hero represents a natural force, if the life

---

David, and of the Messiah, reconstitute the name of the first man; or that Abraham is mineral life; Isaac is vegetable life; Jacob is animal life; David is soul life; Solomon is intellectual life. All these and other details are mere curiosities, being seemingly devoid of any direct relationship with the dual reality of action and prayer—so we only mention them in passing.

[2] Let us note, finally, with Topinard (*Annales de la Société d' Anthropologie*, 1883), with de Lafont and Bunsen, that if Moses married the daughter of Jethro the Kenite, Judah the Chananean Thamar, and Boaz the Moabite Ruth—then David was not of pure Jewish race, and neither was Christ. The Galileans and the Samaritans were Medo-Persian immigrants; the Galileans of today resemble the Poles; at the time of Abraham there were already browns and blonds in Palestine. The tradition that implies that Jesus was blond has some truth in it.

of each prophet dramatizes the flight of one of the spiritual faculties of the human being, if each warrior of Israel symbolizes one of our faculties of action, if each book retraces one of the spires of universal life—if all this be so, let us with the most peaceful, immovable, and deepest certitude also know that the knowledge of these mysteries (for the conquest of which so many men have consumed their energies), that these precious arcana, are for us humble servants of the Friend as a handful of sand in the palm of a child. The little fingers do not know how to close, so the brilliant sand filters away, returning to the shore from which it was taken a moment before.

The knowledge attained by the disciples of Christ is greater, far more substantial and precious, than all the truths extracted with great pains through the combined efforts of gods and men. This effort is admirable, but the least glance that the Father sheds upon us communicates infinitely greater gifts.

⊕

These two genealogies give us an inkling as to the importance of names. The practitioners of occultism and the liturgists recognize this also.

The Father sows souls by the handful: they incarnate in groups, they travel in tribes and radiate the light that was entrusted to them. The members of the same group have a similar task, since they cross the same regions. They wear the same insignia, since they employ the same faculties. They are led as a herd under the surveillance of a shepherd and his dogs. However, few among men are really aware of the presence of the dogs, and rarer still are those who have sighted the high stature of the Shepherd.

Our guides need a sign by which to recognize each of us.

The Genealogy of Jesus

That sign is our name. Our first name, common or aristocratic, hides a mystery. Neither gematria, hieroglyphics, the science of incantations, nor philology give us any information about the true value of a first name.

These sciences contain singular truths, but they remain approximate. They offer bizarre recipes, often efficacious, but that belong to the sphere of human wisdom—it is magic, it is part of the world of wonders, it does not belong to the supernatural, divine world. They are processes by means of which a current of some kind of force gears itself upon the current immediately above it.

In truth, life is one. It is not necessary that a word be written in Sanskrit, or a sign be Chinese, to contain force. I might even say that it is wrong to ascribe partial sentiments to the Creator: He is good, he does not disinherit his children, He does not neglect any of his work, he has lavished gifts equally everywhere. Each man has within his grasp the most living of forces, and has within reach the rarest of marvels. It is an illusion to seek for them afar.

God is everywhere; truth is everywhere. Let the sages of the world celebrate ancient wisdoms. Let them praise the learned contexts of hierograms. But our simple modern language conceals the highest intellectual mysteries and the purest spiritual force. They admire (and with reason) the startling architecture of the rites of antiquity. But he who has taken the trouble to study without preconceived ideas our dogma, our liturgy, our sacred arts, is surprised to discover that they contain all the mysteries of ancient religions, and more besides. How artificial do the Hermetic initiations seem to one who has had the courage to renounce all that is not Christ, and whom our Friend embraces at times in his merciful arms!

Each time a creature enters into a world, its primal name is translated into the language of this new sojourn. Because each of these births, which are initiations, is sanctified by a purifying baptism, the ceremony is not always celebrated physically. But it always takes place.

On this earth, for example, the child who is presented at the baptismal font is already baptized in the invisible. His godfather, godmother, and parents believe they had free choice of names, but they are mistaken. An angel suggested it to them—in particular, the one they will use was irresistibly imposed.

The first name will be the particular sign of this child, the whole length of his existence, visible and invisible, by which the conducting, protective, and tempting elemental spirits will recognize him and will shed upon him prayers or tests.

As to his essential name, God alone knows it, and he communicates it only to the Virgin and to the mysterious being who on earth fills the function of the Word, because the knowledge of the true name of a being confers upon this being who knows it an absolute power, and only that one upon whom all eternal light reposes is capable of never abusing that power.[3]

---

[3] At this point, the esotericist may want to study the Kabbalah, the *Shemhamphorasch*, and the Hindu *mantra*; he may want to analyze the litanies and rosaries of Brahmanism, Lamaism, Sufism, and Catholicism. He will meditate along with Arbatel: "The one to whom God has revealed the names of creatures will know the true virtues and the nature of things, the order and harmony of all visible and invisible creation"; with Pierre d'Aban: "He who knows the real name of a being has command over him"; and with Dr Marc Haven: "In magic, one begins by

The Genealogy of Jesus

⊕

The science of comparative religions cannot explain all the difficulties that had to be overcome so that the coming of such a being as Christ could become a possibility. If one thinks of him as an adept, the preparatory work of Moses is disproportionate to the aim pursued. But if we believe him—Christ—to be the only Son of God, we are surprised that the energies of Israel, which so often vacillated, were able to hew out the indispensable foundations for the vertiginous edifice of the gospel.

We cannot visualize the dazzling magnificence of eternal life. To do so, we would have to use comparisons such as those that concern astronomical grandeurs. As you know, there exist in the Beyond a great many beings with incandescent hearts, at whose proximity our bodies and homes would burn. And there are others who do not permit themselves to approach the frontiers of our solar system because the eddies of their flight would upset even the course of the planets. If ever at the extremities of the horizon you have been able to see the flamboyant silhouette of one of these gods, you will understand why the Church declares the coming of the Word an inaccessible mystery. And yet, his incarnation was but the last link of an immense web of miracles. Because, just as the infinite is as far from the number three as it is from a numerical figure of twenty numbers, so is the Word as far beyond a grain of sand as it is beyond the Milky Way. His aeonian descent into incar-

---

using the virtue of spirits; then, through prayer, are revealed the names in *El* that are transitory and rarely last beyond forty years; then the names in *Yah*." May the student not be bogged down into the quagmire he will find during his explorations!

nation through denser and denser spaces is truly an "innumerable," incomprehensible sequence. Also: how did all these creatures who had received one glance from the Son of God continue to live? What about the stones on the path and all the other things he touched? How were they able to resist blazing up at the proximity of this incandescent Love?

The story of the Jewish people is the story of a corner of terrestrial life preparing for this divine descent. All the books of Israel were but a preface to eternal words.

The army of stars is a living organism. A planet does not remain riveted to the same cosmic function from its birth to its death. It plays several roles. It receives and distributes different forces according to the temporal cycles it passes through. It can serve as habitat to diverse creatures, since it finds itself becoming various crossroads in the complicated system of the roads of the universe. Just as one little elemental spirit today animates a cell of our intestines and in a few years will animate another cell of our lungs or of our brain, so, in turn, each planet fulfills the role of illuminatrix in the universe. Ours, twenty centuries ago, was such a one.

The earth at that time was the place of universal rendezvous. All the authorized representatives of all the races of created beings had to be there. All the roads through which the gods, the elementals, men, beasts, ideas, substances, and forces had to descend had to be opened to this mass immigration. Everything in the universe holds together, and thousands of years were hardly sufficient to organize the reunion of so many travelers.

Among other preparations, it was essential that some few among men be dedicated to the construction of a sojourn worthy of the dignity of the Messiah in the physical domains of life. Some localities had to be reserved so as to

The Genealogy of Jesus

recapture, by concentrating, the ebbing efforts of patriarchal civilizations, in order to sublimate the family, the economic, intellectual, and religious dynamics: a society where itinerant preachers would be possible, a cult uniquely monotheistic, a science founded only upon the observance of the invisible, a people loving positive, concrete life (i.e., not metaphysically inclined, passionate but not intellectual). The penetrating force that Christ was to bring on earth could only be deposited into a chalice carved out of the most inalterable matter.

What a magnificent endeavor it would be to examine again the Pentateuch, the Psalms, the Solomonic books, and the Prophets, plus all the secret work of spiritual preparations that permitted the tree of Jesse to germinate. I do not wish to undertake such a commentary. Years would be needed, and it would take us away from our actual duty, which is our one indispensable effort. Another great endeavor would be to trace within the two genealogies of Christ the steps of the soul, from its departure from heaven until its landing—and from its present state back to the day of its first apparition on earth. We can only hope that on the day the defense of the Christic tradition makes this study necessary, the scholars, thinkers, and apologists required to that purpose will be raised up.

Were we to know the biography of each of these terrestrial ancestors of Christ, we would see the overall picture of the same process by which individual regeneration is prepared. In both cases, the creature (whether the elect people or the chosen disciple) develops—by trial, purification, repentance, penance—the qualitative "negations" contrary to yet analogous to the active virtues that will be fomented by the lighted Christic spark. Thus Jesus radiated in purity all the love that David exhales from the depth of the mire where he was. Jesus really possessed in himself and in his nature the knowledge of which Solomon had to slowly conquer the occult reflection thereof. Jesus practiced, in love and kindness, all the powers that Moses could only conquer bits of and that he deployed according to rigor. This is the complete opposite of physiological heredity. Since Adam, the race that had been selected in Israel had to carve out the mold from which the divine metal was to take form and to position the negative pole as irresistible evocator of the positive.

The one important thing is to extract from the life of our God examples for our life. While perusing the Good Book let us persuade ourselves that the one work, the great work, the work of art, is to have Jesus come into us as he came in the beginning and as he came on earth two thousand years ago—and if his scrupulous biographers have taken pains to enumerate rather obscure terrestrial ancestors so carefully, it must mean something.

What this means from our chosen standpoint is that never will Jesus be born in us unless we have aforetime elaborated the little domain that constitutes our personality to that end through numerous lives, some on earth, some beyond earth. It means that this slow purification of our being includes all of its departments, from the radiant organisms of our superior unconscious down to our flesh, even to the marrow of our bones. It means that this purification occurs all along the spirals of cosmic evolution by means of the dual and parallel work of our universal self (of which Adam is the figuration) and of the planetary self (which David represents exactly). If we need not know the details of this immense enterprise, at least we must know

The Genealogy of Jesus

how much pathos is in the drama of this new birth, how much anguish, weeping, effort, and martyrdom it demands; how precious it is, and how really indescribable and inconceivable to our present state of consciousness.

Finally, what we must know is that just as the ancestors of Christ did nothing but prepare (in the physical, familial, social, religious, intellectual, occult, and spiritual atmospheres of this earth) clean chambers to receive the Word, so our pains, sorrows, illnesses, fatigues, undertakings, gifts, wills, and desires only make ready (in each of the inner apartments of which we are constituted) equally clean chambers and chalices pure enough to receive our Jesus.

No more than the God-child possessed in himself anything that came from heredity, atavism, education, or his surroundings, neither will the eternal light that will be lit in us be related to the least molecule of our actual being.

Nature, cosmic or human, is unable to do anything else but make itself open to receive. It cannot do violence to God.

I ask you, in order that you may enter entirely into the spirit of abandonment, confidence, and humility that is the very spirit of the gospel, to make the effort for the truth of this axiom to become a reality in you as of this very moment—that we are useless servants and according to absolute justice do not have any merit. It is only love that gives us some measure of merit, though we are unworthy. So, do enter into love, and may nothing ever make you step out from this translucid, pacific, and living world.

John the Baptist

NASMUCH AS many have undertaken to write the story of those things, whose truths have always been believed among us, even as they who taught them to us were witnesses from the very beginning and ministers of the Word; it seemed good to me, most excellent Theophilus, to write them down in order, after having been informed exactly of their origin, that you might know the certainty of those things wherein you have been instructed.

There was, in the days of Herod the King of Judea, a certain priest named Zacharias, of the priestly division of Abia; his wife was of the daughters of Aaron, and her name was Elizabeth. They were both righteous before God, walking in all the commandments and ordinances of the Lord in a blameless manner. They had no child, because Elizabeth was barren, and they both were now elderly. It came to pass, that while he executed the priest's office before God, in the order of his duty, according to the custom of the priest's office, his lot was to burn incense when he went into the temple of the Lord. The whole multitude of the people were praying without at the time of incense. There appeared unto him an angel of the Lord standing on the right side of the altar of incense, and when Zacharias saw him he was troubled, and fear fell upon him, but the angel said unto him, Fear not, Zacharias: for thy prayer is heard; and thy wife Elizabeth shall bear thee a son, and thou shalt call his name John. Thou shalt have joy and gladness; and many shall rejoice at his birth, for he shall be great in the sight of the Lord, and shall drink neither wine nor strong drink; and he shall be filled with the Holy Spirit, even from his mother's womb. Many of the children of Israel shall he turn to the Lord their God. And he shall go before him in the spirit and power of Elijah, to reawaken the hearts of the fathers within the children, and bring the disobedient to the wisdom of the just so as to make ready a people prepared for the Lord.

Zacharias said unto the angel, Whereby shall I know this? For I am an old man, and my wife well stricken in years. And the angel answered him, I am Gabriel, that stands in the presence of God: and am sent to speak unto thee, and to announce these glad tidings. Behold, thou shalt be dumb, and not able to speak, until the day that these things shall be performed, because thou believed not my words, which shall be fulfilled in their season.

The people waited for Zacharias, and marveled that he tarried so long in the temple. When he came out, he could not speak unto them; and they perceived that he had seen a vision in the temple: for he beckoned unto them, and remained speechless. It came to pass, that, as soon as the day of his ministration was accomplished, he departed to his own house and after those days his wife Elizabeth conceived, and hid herself five months, saying, Thus hath the Lord dealt with me in the days wherein he looked on me to take away my reproach among men. (Luke 1:1–25)

Now Elizabeth's full time came, and she brought forth a son. Her neighbors and cousins heard how the Lord had shown great mercy upon her; and they rejoiced with her. Now it came to pass, that on the eighth day they came to circumcise the child; and they wanted to call him Zacharias, after the name of his father. But his mother answered and said, Not so; he shall be called John. They said unto her, There is none of thy kindred that is called by this name. They made signs to his father, how he would have him called. And he asked for a writing table and wrote, his name is John. And they all marveled. His mouth was opened immediately, his tongue loosed, then he spoke, and praised God. Fear came on all that dwelt around; and all these sayings were divulged throughout all the hill country of Judea. All they that heard them laid up in their hearts, saying What manner of child shall this be? Because the hand of the Lord was with him. (Luke 1:57–66)

Let us now examine the embassy of the Invisible. It is directed towards Judea, kingdom of Herod. Physically, Judea is the foyer of infernal ardors. Mystically, it is the summit over which the breath of mystery passes. Herod governs Judea, the land of ontological principles. There, incognito, lives a couple whose grandeur comes from their silence and submission. The husband is Zacharias. He bears the name of his office: "the sacrificer," "the male." He ranks with Abia, the "father of the Lord," and is of the race of

John the Baptist

David the beloved. His wife, Elizabeth, is also of the sacerdotal race of Aaron. Aaron means "inhabitant of the summits." Elizabeth means "the queen of the septenary," or "the house of Elijah" (also "the oath of the Most High")—while, by the same cipher, the name of her husband may be read as "the memory of the Creator."

Let us here, in wonder, admire how the coding expected since the beginning of the world, predicted by the very promise of God, is finally being incarnated by these two old married people just before its realization. This is not symbolism. It is the fulfillment of divine words.

The Father conceives, thinks, imagines, and decrees (words are incapable of explaining the mode of the Lord's activity), and his volitions effect their trajectory by fecundating (if I might express it so) the organic substance of each world they go through, and by taking body in living forms. Can anyone compute how many centuries the love of the Father, wanting to save this earth, used to move its soul of granite and extract from it the cells of good will with which the bodies of the parents of the Precursor had to be built? In short, this primal promise that the Father made to men to reconcile himself with them one day, was thrown into the cosmic mass as one of those active ferments that, in the bosom of an organic liquid, works, becomes active, multiplies, and ends by transforming the entire character of that milieu. The promise of the Father that permeates through armies of all creatures comes and goes, spending itself, even seeking the beings it can use—and finally succeeds in building for itself a perfect expression in each of the milieux from the ensemble of which the universe is composed.

Zacharias and Elizabeth were for our earth the realization

of the promise of divine forgiveness: he, incarnating as the angel of repentance; she, incarnating as the voice of the conscience. Let us remember that the words of God create in the self as well as in the non-self; and that they create by fomenting their analogical opposites in the milieu through which they pass. Thus, the promise above evokes within the human spirit the awareness of his sin. And the registering of this promise in the Book of Life engenders in us a desire for perfection.

Zacharias and his wife fill the role of precursors, and I find them not only in history, not only at the end of the solitary road upon which the Baptist appears, but also in the heart of each man. Within this red sun I see a lofty trinity: John the Baptist, the penitent who ploughs and stirs; son of Elizabeth (she of repentance, so long sterile); and son of the perfumed Zacharias (whose desires for divine things rise up to the canopy of the Temple).

These two are old, because many incarnations are needed for the self to turn to the Light. But behind this grouping of hope and expectation I discover another of certitude and of victory—the slumbering spark of the Word, the regenerating Jesus. By this I mean Mary (inexhaustible source of grace, the all-pure, the elect) and Joseph (the self grown old from labors, renunciations, and strife). We will often find that the gospel story thus unfolds its ballad through the triple and parallel development of cosmic salvation. We can discover in the conjunction of these two ternary groups certainly the most spiritual method, and a key to all doors of the inner castles.

Every father of a family should be as Zacharias was—pontiff in his home. A family is a collective being. The husband is the visible head. He has the authority. His wife has the power. Couples are responsible for all that nature has entrusted to them. They are even responsible for the child who is born to them, and whose spiritual quality depends a great deal upon their morality. Atavism and heredity are not causes, but effects. The frail child is not born thus because his parents are degenerate; rather, he came to them because he merited such a pathological stigma.

The observances of ancient sages relative to marriage made perfect sense. Actually, it has become impossible to enforce them, since the conditions of the spiritual milieu have been upset from top to bottom. Yet we can demand assistance in any of our life's endeavors. And were we to observe these precautionary measures, it would spare us many a mishap.

No one is alone in the universe. When a soul comes to this earth, it is led. Moreover, signs of the approaching benediction are given to the parents if they have eyes to see and ears to hear. These signs are given by a being who manifests himself only in extraordinary circumstances. And at the same time a multitude of spirits, who are inferior to man and come from physical nature and from elsewhere, also pray. The birth of a man is for them a happy event, as we human beings are their sun and their guide.

Thus, all is of grave import in life, and the smallest happenings have far-reaching repercussions. They represent joy to some, unhappiness for others—but should be lessons for all.

So, one day Zacharias went to the Perfume Altar to perform his ministry. According to St John Chrysostom, it was during the period of fasting in September that Gabriel appeared to him. It was Gabriel—the archangel of force, the giant of God, the governor of Septentrion, "the north"

—who announced to Zacharias the birth of a son. Yes! To him, the old man, and to his sterile wife. This son was a predestined soul. Predestination! How this word shocks the pride of man! Yet we are all predestined. To each of us providence opens a road at the end of which lies a paradise, a state of being where all our powers will unfold in beatitude. According to this understanding, man is predestined.

Our work at this time, however, is to obey. By means of this obedience we move towards the conquest of our liberty. Considering humanity as a whole, one observes that the Father had given to the Jews, a minority people, a superabundance of truths. Those people, the hardest and most indocile, threw them over, prostituted and deformed them; and these lights that they had refused were accepted by others less favored with celestial gifts. These latter bettered themselves, and by their amendment provoked the amelioration of the impenitent race.

In the spirit of man, the strongest faculties, such as those of the heart, follow the same process and receive the lights in full. And when they likewise reject them, the secondary faculties receive the lights. When the assimilation is in full course, these faculties cause reactions in the others. Thus is man saved after slow transformations.

You see now why the terms "elect" and "rejected" must be taken in a transitory sense. Predestination is the goddess who exerts upon us a decreasing influence. We escape her tyranny in proportion to the measures wherein we have submitted to her graciously.

No one is predestined to unhappiness. Sorrow only makes us suffer because we refuse our providential destiny. So, this unexpected child, about whom everything, even his very name and other things had been predestined, will be

John the Baptist

called John, which means "the favorite of the creator" and "perfection of grace."

The son of Zacharias brings joy to his father and to others—both living and dead—because he is the fulfillment of divine promises and of the tenacious hopes for which these just men consumed their lives. Thus, within each of us, there are beings, cells, and forces athirst for the eternal dawn until their last agony. But as soon as our heart turns towards God, understands him, imagines him, and tries to be assimilated by him, then these unknown inhabitants of our spirit rush to our aid with all the strength of their resuscitated forces, with all the reborn ardor of their former consumptions.

The great explorers of mystical deserts, the Fathers of the Thebaid, the staunch supporters of Catholicism such as Loyola, the isolated laics such as Boehme, teach—one and all—that our will (which means, our love) must sculpt within us, through a purgative life of asceticism and penance, the greatest image of the Word that we can conceive. But at the end of this slow labor within the crypts of solitude and silence, when our strength is ebbing, when night is at its darkest, when desolation disassociates our constitutive elements, this very pure chalice we will have become, this insignificant and inalterable vase, will be filled by the Word—filled with the eternal water that sets us ablaze, that illumines and regenerates us.

This is one of the reasons that will cause the Precursor to later state: "He must increase, but I must decrease." Because it is in the diminishing of the self-filled-by-the-self that the true grandeur of man may be measured. Thus it is that the Baptist is great in the eyes of God. Also, it was he alone who among humanity received the unique honor of

THE CHILDHOOD OF JESUS

being praised by an angel and by Jesus. How can we ever sound the depth of these tributes? The Church has recognized that this man is the first among men. Yet he remained in the background. Barely a few thousand people ever heard him speak. He spent his entire life within a small territory. It is because (just as it was with the Virgin, the only one besides him whose birth is celebrated) his grandeur was entirely within. The partisans of the theory of the solar myth have underscored in favor of their system the parallel or opposites of St John's Feast, June 24, with Christmas, December 24. But there is a more mysterious teaching that the calendar devisers probably ignored, and we will mention it again. Before this child was able to stand by himself, he was already in daily contact with the Invisible; his heart and intelligence were already ablaze with ardor, desire, and thoughts which were radiating from him. No matter how unbelievable such a childhood may seem, it is possible. Many other examples are known, and I have been witness to a similar one. The direct envoy of the Father in fact begins his work from the moment of his birth. He may not be able to talk yet, but already the flame burning within him heals and accomplishes miracles. But remember that this only occurs in the case of an immediate filiation of the Father, in the case of one "re-descended" from heaven.

The evangelist calls our attention to this individual. He specifies that John the Baptist will drink neither wine nor strong drink. Wine belongs to the psychic regimes of ancient initiations, to the subtle essence or emanation of cosmic life that the adepts knew how to assimilate. All the mystagogues worthy of the name (whether traditional or not) knew how to make use of those processes. There are various sorts of messengers. Some are guided by inspiration

John the Baptist

only: it is the gods who speak to them and guide them. Others receive the gods themselves, incarnating them. Upon the personality of these latter a supraterrestrial entity grafts himself, on which account their followers elevate them to the level of gods. But the veritable messenger is he whose message seems total and remains permanent—such a one is an emissary of the Father. That individual keeps his entire liberty. God does not touch his individuality. He only gives him a new force, and a "virgin secret." This secret will be the origin of all the thaumaturgic works of this "re-descended" one.

"Strong drink" (cervoise, a kind of beer) represents the muddy exhalations of the spirit of this world, of the stars, of the elements that all men seek and from which the intoxication dunks them so often in the mire. But John's foster-father is the Spirit. The word Spirit really means nothing to us. We live unconscious and somnolent. We do not even understand why Jesus recommends that we watch. We are a fallow land where rodents thrive. And if at times we plant a meager hedge, it is usually at the very place where the plough of the divine Laborer could enter.

We think of divine realities as abstractions. What does it mean to be "fed by the Spirit"? Do we who fancy ourselves "positive" people believe that intelligence, truth, prayer, wisdom, science, force, and love—these gifts of the Consoler—are really living substances and eternal beings? Yet many of the poor of God know it, since at the sound of their voice catastrophes are averted, illness departs, courage is reawakened among the sufferers.

But rarer are those who are "filled with the Holy Spirit." A mystic will hardly find one each century on earth. Their personality has undergone the severest purification. Were the wisest among us to receive from the Spirit one single imperceptible breath, everything in them would be shattered: their will would go to the right, their thoughts to the left, their lives would vanish in smoke, and their bodies be reduced to ashes.

To be filled with the Spirit really means having constant omniscience, immediate omnipotence. It means being free, since "the Spirit blows where he wills..." It also means asking Satan as well as a stone for their secret, and doing so in such a tone of voice that neither the gigantic archangel nor the inert silica may evade the answer. It means speaking with the Father. It means ordering a comet, a continent, or even death. It also means having suffered, obeyed, and loved for so long that God grants in advance all the demands and ratifies all the decisions of his child.

These are just a few qualifications necessary to the work of "bringing back" the erring ones. If Jesus is the good shepherd, dare I say that John the Baptist is his faithful, tireless, and vigilant sheep dog? Please understand how I mean this. There is a mystery in all domestic animals, but in the sheep dog are many mysteries. Have you ever looked at the eyes of a sheep dog? Have you noticed all that can be seen in their touching pupils? You will find devotion, joy of serving, worry, anguish, also humble resignation, even the humble ecstasy of adoration.

But to come back to our subject. Only such a man "walks straight ahead" or "straight towards the Lord." Creation is his. We, too, walk, since we exist; but our "march" is slow, irregular, and hesitant. We make mistakes, retrace our steps. We drag along because we do not see our duty. Or else, if aware of it, we do not care to accomplish it. John and his spiritual brothers alone know how to walk straight ahead without faltering, without error—while as unknown as they wish to be—because God, with whom their union has been made, is the most unknown of all. They also triumph if they deem it necessary. This existence is in itself a dare to all laws of nature and a mystery to the sages who often pass right by them without perceiving their presence. The spirit who saturates them exudes an arch-mysterious halo around them. Ordinary men, the drinkers of the symbolic "strong drink" see nothing out of the ordinary about them—sometimes they are even scandalized by their actions, whose motives to them remain undecipherable.

But if someone who suffers for the light meets one of these elect, he suddenly has the presentiment that hidden treasures lie beneath the appearance of a man who seems so familiar to all others, but whose rich voice echoes the mysterious, whose unfathomable eyes project superhuman lights. Here we are faced with an inner drama that even tongues cannot explain, because in so doing we have prostituted our speech. The mystical writers keep silent about the definitive dialogues that the soul exchanges with its Friend.

The son of Elizabeth "will walk in the spirit and in the virtue of Elijah." There are forms of language that would reveal many mysteries to us, were we to accept them ingenuously. Why should the existence of a man, his actions, the events he provokes and suffers, the states of soul he elaborates—why should the Holy Writings call them a "walk"? Because, remember, a symbol *per se* is non-existent: a symbol is always a *reality*.

Creatures roam the world: all the vital centers of the cosmos, all the planets visible and invisible, objective and subjective, are connected one to another by paths. There are paths or roads everywhere. Have you ever wondered, as you walked along, why the fig tree's grayish branches are entangled like a serpent's nest? Why the olive tree twists its branches like the knotted limbs of an athlete? Why the poplar rises straight while the chestnut tree spreads spherically? It is because each branch, each twig, each bough or leaf, sees its particular path in the atmosphere. The tree does not construct itself cell by cell merely by means of the food extracted from the soil. Rather, each atom of strength that beads upon the extremity of a sprig must search for the point in the atmosphere where passes the particular magneto-telluric currents assimilable for it. And when the junction of these two infinitesimals takes place, a material cell is added to the sprig.

The directions according to which metallic ores increase, and their veins expand, in the entrails of the earth, obey the same laws. So do the physical forms of animals. Water, blood, chlorophyll follow invisible beds. Ideas and people too. Spirits, material or human, have invisible roads. Planets, events, cosmic forces, and creatures all march along. And amidst this infinitely complicated network of paths the Spirit reopens, at intervals, a transversal road, one that has been forgotten for centuries.

Men go in groups from one world to another. Sometimes these groups are multitudes, and so they take the wide, flat roads that are easy and slow. At times, these groups are comprised of but a hundred, or but a dozen people. The path is then more arduous, but shorter. Finally, there are within invisible savannas almost hidden footpaths that cross chases, scale peaks, cut straight through marshes and forests, where you never meet another soul. These solitary footpaths

John the Baptist

are frightful and filled with lairs, but are faster. They permit our crossing magnificent and moving landscapes. At long intervals, some intrepid traveler takes them. Like the Precursor, he marches straight ahead, wears himself out. Tortured by hunger and thirst, and also by fear, he advances nonetheless. He knows his sufferings will prove useful. A few centuries hence, this perilous trace will become a broad highway filled with peaceful travelers who will bring life, wealth, and civilization where before was nothing but solitude. Such was the path chosen by John the Baptist.

Remember that his journey is not over. And if your souls—freed, persevering, untiring—could go beyond the gates of the earth, you would doubtless see upon the road that leads to the sun this same half-naked traveler whose voice reverberated for centuries across invisible deserts, that resounded for thirty years in the deserts of Judea, and that men will hear once more with terror during the days of the last ordeals.

But, you might be thinking, if Christ is the Master, he needs no one to prepare his coming. That is true. He himself anticipated it since the first movement of creation, and began preparing himself. But humanity, agonizingly sick, could only take a remedy proportionate to its weakened condition and slow action. First the desire for getting well had to be awakened, otherwise no salvation was possible. That was the work of the prophets. But their light was only a shadow of the Light. To prepare the world to receive the divine remedy, a Friend became essential—one who had learned over a long period of time how to speak with the patient and who knew the supernatural virtue of the medicament.

Elijah

ET US NOW look at the figure of Elijah rising before us. Greater than the greatest sages, freer than the all-powerfuls, initiated not by men, not by the invisible, but by the Spirit, this solitary traveler spreads his miracles across Israel from Lebanon to Edom.

Who is he? He keeps silent about himself, and this makes him tower above the highest among superhumans. I have tried to explain to you one of the conceptions we might have of his better known personality: that of John the Baptist. Let us, by means of a rapid survey of his prior existence, try to discover its profound roots.

He came the first time to sow aloft, upon the summits, among the sands, and in the hearts of gods, the devastating seeds of fear. He came a second time so that the worlds, the abysses, and the firmaments might not see the Light just yet, but instead the reflection of its brilliance, so that the leaders might cease their tyranny over the weak, so that the powerful might recognize something more powerful. And he will return a third time for the last, terrible harvest.

Do you remember the extraordinary circumstances of the mission of the Tishbite? He appears all of a sudden in the Chronicles of the Kings without anything to announce him, or to motivate him. He attacks idolatries; he has command over the elements; he conquers death. The resurrection of the son of the widow of Zarephath is the first

Elijah

triumph of man over the Reaper. Elijah is simple and incomprehensible. He is one, yet he shows disconcerting contrasts. Thus this naked solitary, this dismal vagabond who practices effortlessly, without any preparation, the powers of the highest adepts, who overthrows kings and emblazes their followers with one word; this master of the air, this master over disease, this master of the gods—this man whose life is a continuous miracle is menaced by Jezebel. He trembles and runs away, not knowing where to hide. He groans with fear. Let that startling spectacle be a perpetual lesson to our pride. When divine power took its hand away from this man, he fell down.

How shall we understand this? James the Apostle will state a long while afterward: "Elijah was a man subject to like passions as we are." Initiatory words! Strength within weakness, power of humility, mystery of eternal decrees!

This is a new occasion for pointing out the mode of relationships that God maintains with us.

Do take a look at Elijah. He is truly unique. He surpasses the most extraordinary men; he frightens us; we hardly believe what is told about him. Yet this prestigious power is but an addition to his self. It does not belong to him, since Jezebel can annul it.

Do you not see how the Father looked at Israel and judged how this people needed to be whipped? How he chose a man who possessed certain powers and gave him the rods and told him: "Lash them"? But the lashes—meaning the powers of the thaumaturge—do not belong to him. Even the strength of his arm, though seemingly his, is not permanent. An unforeseen shock may check it. And yet, how much suffering did his soul have to undergo in order to sustain the ardor of the torch he was ordered to brandish over Israel? Let us conclude: we are useless servants. We must work, we must wear ourselves out and be consumed. Yet we must understand that all these sorrows would never give us anything to do with justice, were love not to intervene. Know that, and you will understand the formidable solitary of Mount Carmel.

After this frightful crisis, which must have devastated the soul of Elijah just as the famine had devastated the Hebraic land, he became again the man his name signifies: the master, the powerful.

An angel fed him and sent him to Mount Horeb—forty days' march away from the desert to which he had fled. Forty is the number of penance and expiation. The word Horeb means: vision, occident, hell, or raven, according to the accent applied. Let us transport ourselves in thought to this majestic peak. Let us behold the large bare rocks that raise their heads above the rustling forests, the luxuriant gardens, and overhead the sky-blue sea. Do look up there, and see the tiny silhouette of the naked ascetic who stands upright awaiting a sign from God. Beneath the flame that sets this man afire, the earth begins to quake. The mountain trembles. The tempest uproots the cedars and shatters the rock walls. The ravines turn into cascades. Lightning bolts fall. But amidst this fracas of the elements unleashed, the heart of our solitary sees nothing in it but an upheaval from the gods, and so these convulsions affect him not. What were then his thoughts?

In order to guess, one must join with one of his direct sons, twenty centuries later: a monk kneeling in the dilapidated cell of a miserably poor Spanish convent; a threadbare Carmelite, ill, worn, yet burning with the most intense ardor, the hardiest of all Catholic contemplatives—I mean

Elijah

St John of the Cross. One must read over his pages of *The Ascent of Mount Carmel* to hear the most frightful cries that thirst for the Absolute has ever wrung from a human heart. One must scale the abrupt cliffs of inner destitution, leave behind the most scintillating and beautiful stars of virtue, climb higher and still higher, till—our head afire—we finally reach the frightful darkness where only the supernatural breath of the Spirit blows.

There, and only there, will we enjoy the savor of the bible stories; there will we re-live the tempest on Mount Horeb, the sudden calm after the storm, and the wafting breath slowly drifting into the infinite silence that suddenly sets in.

The prophet is not mistaken. To him this breath foretells the Infinite Presence; and only then does he bow, immersed in adoration.

How I regret not being able to tell you how powerful this scene was, except in my humble words, and how, from it, the unexplainable undulates as high waves.

Enjoy the sweetness, the grace, the tenderness of this fresh breath. It is the forerunner of Joseph, of the welcoming Christ, of the Friend who will carry our load upon his powerful shoulders. If, when praying, a sacred ardor transports you from this world, remember that such dazzlements, such transports of joy and thunder, are not from heaven. Heaven is a tremor, a breath, an imperceptible touch in the bottom of your heart. You are moved, bathed in a supernatural freshness, filled with certitude, overflowing with kindness, ready to bear everything and to undertake anything: such is the mode of eternal life.

But let us come back to Elijah. He continues his march as a thaumaturge. He anoints kings, takes Elisha away from his plough, avenges Naboth, handles lightning bolts. Finally, his saga ends on the most extraordinary fact (which had only happened twice before): when God recalls his servant to him, death dare not touch him; the entrails of the earth dare not claim that body. Elijah is taken to heaven in a manner similar to the flashing forth of Enoch and Moses. Meanwhile, his disciple Elisha assumes the mantle of his master, both his spirit and his virtue. Such an assumption indicates a soul ready to quit this universe definitively. Elijah had already surpassed the highest adepts. The earth had no more rights upon him. Hence it is quite natural that when he returned as the Precursor, Christ saluted him as the greatest among the sons of men.

The positive intuition of people of the East affirms his survival and his return. In fact, that which is characteristic of a reincarnation is not the resumption of the same material cells, but the identity of the "spirit": the complex organism whose core is the self. Characteristic of reincarnation is also the perpetuation of the same "virtue": the power proportionate to the efforts and to the works accomplished. Because, even if some among us, perhaps with greater knowledge, accept reincarnation, nonetheless they still only comprehend one phase of it, of which there are in truth many. So let us leave these premature researches aside.

A few months before the birth of his Master, John comes down again to earth with the "spirit" and the "virtue" he had previously possessed.

All the solicitudes, the silent exhortations and ardent hopes of the ancient righteous of Israel, and of the venerable group that for centuries, and from the extremities of the world, have called for the Savior, descend simultaneously— all the righteous that no physical idols or mental idols have

Elijah

ever been able to seduce, all those who remained steadfast in their confidence and unity. Because of them, Christ gives himself the title, so full of love, of "Son of Man." The frightening Elijah, under the guise of the Precursor, is the individualization and embodiment of this great, obstinate clamor, this "voice that cries in the wilderness." He brings along with him the tonic aroma of invisible solitude and of spiritual summits. He seems to be in revolt and appears independent. That is why he can call together all insubordinations. In fact, he draws them to him because he carries within himself the very placid water of compassion that will transmute the innumerable anarchies of matter, of society, of intelligence, and of desires.

"To make the heart of the fathers relive in their children, to bring rebels back to the wisdom of the just, to prepare a people to accept the Lord"—this triple enterprise is the work of John the Baptist, and it is extremely arduous.

First of all, the wheel of generations that adulteries and idolatries have deformed, arrested, and mixed, must be reorganized. There has to be a search, among souls ready for incarnation, for those who once yearned for the Messiah. We must run after the erring sheep in order that they may of themselves return to the fold, pry into the obscure regions of the Invisible, redress intelligences, transmute wills. We must probe into the various stages of social organism, oversee the ontological powers, seek favorable occasions for the collective descent of souls. But first we must give of our self, give of our strength, moral courage, and life, without lassitude, without sorrow, without auxiliaries. That is a frightening endeavor. Do you see why the Precursor is the greatest among the sons of man?

Can you ever comprehend his sleepless nights, his days

without food, his heart deprived of friends, his intellect parched for books, his will devoid of any support here-below? Can you ever conceive the intense inner workings of that brain, the long-drawn out calculations, the sudden decisions, his silence, his psychic fatigues, the enormous hopes of that inflamed heart, and his painful falls? See how deeply an ordinary woman who cares for her child or her husband suffers! How much more she would suffer were she to love thousands of children and thousands of husbands! Such was the inner martyrdom of John the Baptist. Such is the true function of the prophet.

⊕

Maybe now you will be able to discern how John the Baptist operates "in the spirit and virtue of Elijah." What does spirit mean? What is virtue? Are they synonymous? No.

Is spirit the psychic atmosphere in which Elijah dwelt? Perhaps. But then what is virtue? Too often the words spirit and soul are used to mean the same thing. Generally, spirit is placed in opposition to matter, and one uses that term based upon this antinomy to qualify man's eternal principle as spirit. The Latin *spiritus*, the Greek *pneuma*, the Hebraic *ruach* are not first principles, they are only correlations, ambiences, surroundings.

The Spirit, say the theologians, proceeds from the Father and from the Son. It is the dual current of love that ties the two divine Persons. It is the most subtle, ineffable Breath. It is the great unknown. "The Spirit blows where he wills, and no one knows whence he comes, nor whence he goes," says the gospel. Protean, mystery, ubiquity, absolute life, perpetual motion, total intelligence—such is the Spirit in the non-Self. Can it be anything else within us? No.

Elijah

Hence, the spirit of man is the milieu wherein the living center and the dead center unite, wherein the light of the Word, and the darkness of the ego unite in mutual love. It is the ensemble of all invisible organisms through which we live, act, understand, and love; it is all that which spreads between the eternal soul and our mental bodies—all the ethers, all the astral and mental bodies. It is the seat of individuality, of liberty, and of responsibility. Please understand that "walking in the spirit of Elijah" means living as Elijah would live: it means incarnating him anew.

The *virtues*, *dynameis*, or *geburah* are active, radiating, and operating forces. *Geburah* and *Gabriel* are two words springing from the same root (*G br*), which suggests the idea of a creative organism, the process whereby what was a seed propagates and becomes a being. The virtue of Elijah is also the power of Elijah. They are his very faculties as a thaumaturge and as a prophet—all that God has added unto him as superhuman, which means all that made Elijah, Elijah.

Just as Elijah was unexpected, so is the Baptist unexpected. Like Elijah, he remains solitary, naked, an ascetic and violent. Just like Elijah, he dares the wildest enterprises. Just like Elijah, he is a thaumaturge, except that his thaumaturgy is higher, since he dares to baptize—otherwise he would be an imposter. Just like Elijah, he challenges the kings. And finally, just like Elijah, an unchaste princess wins an illusory, temporal victory over him.

But you may wonder why I mention events of long ago and what might their application be? How can this penetrate our daily life and our present psychological viewpoint?

To give you an answer, or rather in order not to lose ourselves in theories, I prefer giving you an example: the first that comes to my mind, thoughts I had some time ago. One day, as I was strolling along Mount Turbie by the Gulf of Mont-Agel, a magnificent sun shone over the sea and over the rocks; the mountains were sheets of light and symphonies of color. You know how African-like these landscapes can be, how everything becomes poignant: how the olive groves, the mule-pack paths, the stony roads, and the noble cypresses, are a part of a landscape that moves us! The brilliant calm blue sea, the brownish and greenish tones of the hillsides of Nice, the summits sparkling with snow, the delicate hues of the Ligurian and Provençal hills—are they not an ensemble of beauty, of grandeur, and of peace—the temple of God, his house without walls or roof, limitless, filled with his ineffable Presence?

You are there, kindest of Fathers; but your children—mankind—where are they? Here they are. The august calm is shattered with rifle shots. Around the grandstand, the fashion-conscious society is shooting pigeons for the pleasure of useless killing and for vanity!

And so! All of you who have discovered within yourselves such beauties, sisters of those that nature shows us, your duty is to open the eyes of your brothers upon these forms of harmony.

Be poets of action, artists of spirituality, magicians of eternity. Cultivate your spirit body just as the Greeks cultivated their physical body. Cleanse it, exercise it, give it the habit of noble attitudes. Rise above your own selves, become exalted. Face down your dizziness. Fear not being out of your depth. Let yourselves swoon beneath the diamond-like breaths flowing from the mystical snows. And when in the midst of these transports, turn towards your poor brothers, they who are so close, and yet so far from you: they who are so elegant and powerful according to the wisdom of the earth—yet kill doves for the fun of it!

To amuse themselves is synonymous with running away from themselves. They do harm, they are cruel and silly only because they are cowards. They are afraid of, and dare not face themselves.

You who have heard the echo of divine voices, go to them with the invisible assurance that celestial kindness and human compassion give you. Force them to face themselves. They will often throw you out. Do return, your eyes filled, in spite of yourself, with the light dispensed by the sun of spirits from the Beyond. Your eyes will serve as eloquent exhortations to them, if they still refuse to listen to your voice. Thus, you will have utilized for others a little of that which the Father permits you to see of the shadow of his works.

This is but one aspect of the works of the Precursor. Regarding another aspect, I will illustrate it for you as I saw it when I came down the hill in the play of light and serene atmosphere at the end of the day. On my left the sun gave pale golden and old rose tints to the rock-nipple that the Monegasques call La Justice. There the Romans used to have a town, a fort, and a prison: the gallows remained throughout the Middle Ages. It is in this fierce town that some say Christ one evening on his way to Gaul was incarcerated and brutalized for having defended a tramp. Tradition affirms that eight days later an earthquake destroyed the sinister citadel, chasing out the cruel garrison.

Remaining constant in our credulity, we hold this legend as true. It reveals the root of all the crimes, of all the brigandage and piracy in which Christians and Saracens rivaled for centuries all along the coast. This cortege of evil energies leads to the palaces of Monte Carlo, where all vices, corruption, and the coldest cruelties of this earth come to a focus. And as with individuals, so with countries: physical beauty is almost always a lie, as evil men or a fiendish soul may inhabit it.

Now, the second work of John the Baptist is precisely to establish the accord between the external and the internal. It is by being sincere that we will reach it, "in walking straight to the Lord." Let us, too, be the voices who proclaim loudly words heard mystically. There is always within us an eye that sees and is open to the truth. Let us not build walls of hypocrisy before it. It is difficult to be constantly and totally sincere. Let us start right now.

Open the eyes of your spirit. Do not be like the Romans of old. Know how to recognize the envoy from above, no matter under what guise he presents himself—has he not told us that each man in need is himself? What a saying! How it illumines us and broadens our existence! Keep that saying, make it both your sword and your shield. Then throw yourself into the midst of the fight.

These very things I tell you in part are the ones that the Baptist shouted with his formidable voice into all caverns, upon all heights, in all deserts, for all the multitudes.

⊕

But let us return to the Temple of Jerusalem. Zacharias, standing at the corner of the Altar of Incense, listens and looks at the angelic messenger whose translucid form vibrates upon the penumbra among the colonnades. The faraway, profound, and peculiar voice pronounces the words that, one by one, are converting old cherished dreams into unbelievable realities. This is an extraordinary

Elijah

voice. One can hardly hear it, yet it fills the heart of the old priest as a lion's roar fills adjoining caverns. Zacharias is aware that sometimes angels have made themselves visible to men in the past. But what about this? He could touch this luminous phantom, were he to extend his hand. Why did it come to him? Why on this feast day, when the populace outside is growing impatient? And yet his greatest desires are being formulated by this presence. He must be real, because the large Thebaic marble flagstones are cleaving beneath the diaphanous feet of the athlete-of-God. As he talks, his immaterial, outpouring breath sets the golden plaques on the walls afire, curling their edges. We notice that the sacred vapors of the incense spread out in spiraling scrolls attesting to the visits of the highest Malachim, the angels of Israel.

As Zacharias deliberates, the voice becomes still for a moment, then the calm and tremendous voice rises to pronounce the punishment for his doubt. He will remain mute till the fulfillment of the promise. The old man cowers with fear at the thought that this lack of faith might have prevented the predicted marvels from taking place.

This is the last severity of the ancient covenant. The kingdom of mercy is at hand!

The silence of the father prepares the way for the eloquence of the child. The Baptist, in fact, will be primarily a preacher. Books teach. Speech moves. And John was to sway multitudes.

How much must they who teach and exhort others prepare their ministry in solitude, in fasts, and tears! Call to mind now what was said previously regarding predestination: the flower is the analogical opposite of its root; he who wants to command must first learn how to obey; whoever wants to lead multitudes must like solitude; he who wants to teach must cherish silence; whoever wants to become powerful according to heaven must seem weak according to the earth's values and fast morally more so than physically; whoever wants to spread the healing balms of divine joy upon others must first be steeped long in tears of repentance and in the tribulations of ordeals.

Know also that the gift of faith is to be found in a yet unknown relationship with the sense of hearing. The apostle knows it when he states that "faith comes from the ear." There are within us *natural* faculties: memory, comparison, calculation, and imagination. Everyone knows that their presence is made visible by particularities found in the shape of our faces. The *supernatural* faculties such as faith, true love, and theophany possess points of tangence in our conscience, but also localizations within our physical bodies. The ear will someday be the localization of the spiritual force called faith.

But in order to grasp that tenuous relationship, let us consider that faith is *a priori* nothing but the certitude of the inner divine presence. This presence is called the Word—the Word that is the speech of the Father.

The speech of man is also a word. When an orator gives a mediocre lecture, the audience still may be under a spell for a material cause such as the beauty of his voice, his gestures, etc., or for a psychic cause, such as his personal charisma.

But if a man is not an orator, is one who has never prostituted his speech, has never been a traitor, has never insulted or slandered anyone—whenever that man speaks, his words are magic. They carry a generic force that makes them operative. Such a man can heal, console, and enlighten. This is one of the actions of the Word in us.

It is interesting to note that at baptism, after having let the spirit of the child enter into the Church of Christ, the priest opens his ears.

Thus, when we will have developed the spiritual seed of faith, our mentality will surge forward. We will feel, think, and meditate through unknown processes, according to new methods that at the present time are unimaginable. We will then approach the capital faculty of the Spirit, which is ubiquity.

⊕

We are far from having given all the necessary details about the Precursor. But we want to follow the synoptic gospels step by step. The apparent disjointedness of their narratives conceal some very instructive features. Maybe later I will invite you to seek the mystical motifs of interpolations, of reversals, of chronological differences, and of the divergences of details, from which modernists draw their strongest arguments against the supernatural state of the gospels and of Christ. Such a survey is not a difficult work, it is only a test of patience. As for myself, I wish that we may have the time to undertake it together someday.

The Virgin

O SPEAK OF the Virgin is an overwhelming task. The depth and breadth of the subject equally surpass human intelligence. So many profound books, delightful hymns, and admirable canvases have been inspired by this figure of supernatural charm, that the limits of beauty seem to have been reached definitively, as though no more songs could be composed, and not another word worthy to be spoken could be added in praise of this woman, unique among all women. Yet still, I want to tell you about her. May heaven open for you and permit your seeing, beyond my discourse, the resplendent reality of the mysteries that I see but imperfectly, and perspectives unknown to me.

Today our landscape changes. The bleak magnificence that surrounds the Precursor now gives way to fields of intimate and subtle charm. To feel the fresh ingenuousness, may I ask you to make a new effort towards breathing freely and laying yourself bare?

Up to now, we have perceived the eternal sun through the vigorous foliage of exceptional natures. After all, John the Baptist and Elijah are titans of the cast of the Archangel Michael: kings of effort, athletes of true will. The Virgin, however, personifies the angel of meekness, of innocence, of sorrow. She is not even aware of her beauty. She is the candid clump of flowers hidden by the side of a brook. To discover her, one must walk with downcast eyes. And also,

The Virgin

because our invincible tendency is to appear pompous and to let others know all about ourselves, it is difficult for us to understand this plenipotentiary of humility.

Here, particularly, I need your act of faith if you want my words not to remain mere symbol to you. It is with the Virgin that one truly enters into the supernatural kingdom. It is she who welcomes us at the open gate of God's palace. And we really see her only when we look at her with the superhuman eye of faith.

Once for all, let us realize that all we may discover in the gospels are but isolated glimpses and fragmentary sparks. Let us resign ourselves: we can never acquire here-below anything but scraps of knowledge. Let us resist the common mania of wanting to bind these scraps into a system. Let us be as wise as the positivists in this one sense: note how our scientists in their laboratories, before formulating a theory or a simple hypothesis, adduce experiments and observations by the thousands. Let us imitate their modest reserve. I affirm this to you: the highest synthesis, the vastest theologies and esoteric encyclopedias, even the most complex and ancient ones, are but diamonds scattered in the universal mine of integral knowledge.

In any case, there is but one real way of conceiving, of understanding, and of knowing a creature, whatever it may be, whether concrete or abstract. That is, to enumerate its cogs and wheels in order to find out its origin and deduce its aims. And that is done only by sacrificing yourself for it. This is not paradoxical, but almost physiological.

Any knowledge gathered by the intellect is an outer knowledge. It gives us information regarding the results of the central activity of some creature or other, but does not procure for us the experiential savor of this living center.

Howsoever, the least among mental movements never takes place without a sacrifice. To see an object, it is necessary that some cells within us die. Hence, if we would claim to be able to solve the mystery of a being, to make it one with our own mystery, to incorporate it spiritually with us, how many more things must give up their lives in order to effect this humanization? For veritable knowledge is the precious fruit of the fusion of the object sought with the seeker, an intimate fusion in its essence—practical and real in its mode. It is necessary that I, the would-be knower, first approach this other creature whom I know not, that I sympathize with it, help it, love it, so that finally, by sacrificing myself, by giving of my strength and offering of my virtues, I become one with it.

Then, conquered by my love, it will give itself to me freely. Lightened of all the burden of which I have rid it, free of its chain and ball, since I have riveted it to my own ankle, this creature takes off, leaps forward, overtakes me on the secret paths of the spirits. Since it is climbing to another state of existence, it changes raiments, and I see it at that moment in its essential nudity. This sight is true, total, and profound knowledge into the past, the present, and the future.

But these sacrifices must have been concrete and positive—actions, not intentions only. You notice that I often repeat myself. This is because Christic wisdom can be condensed to a very few formulas, in fact to one: sacrifice. Sacrifice in all its inner and outer modes. Any other method gives but precarious, superficial, or unhealthy results. Knowledge is the daughter of Love.

Jesus alone could speak of his Mother with authority. John the Baptist could give us marvelous descriptions of

The Virgin

her, most of which I fear would remain unappreciated by us. Likewise, the Virgin could reveal to us some of the unknown splendors of her Son, such as she has awakened in the subjective corners of the soul and heart of a few extraordinarily privileged saints.

It is here that the preliminary indications of what the great teaching regarding her existence as Mother of all women must mean to us—to wit, that we must understand that the greatest wonders always occur in the shadow—in the entrails of the earth, in the crypts of a heart, among crowds of anonymous people, in cosmic deserts, in the hidden workshops of the gods, in the undecipherable arcana of providential designs, or in the silent regions where the intensity of life prevents any outward expression. May this awaken humility within us, strengthen our patience, and foment the victorious ardor of faith!

⊕

To give an orderly sequence to the overwhelming store of recollections we have of her, let us first speak of the historical personality of Mary, then of the soul and spiritual roots of this elected one, and finally—supplied with these elementary facts—we will review the gospel text with the more probable hope of understanding it better.[1] In the being of Mary of Nazareth, the divine and the human aspects are interwoven with intervals. To describe such a

---

[1] There is innumerable bibliographic material on the Virgin. Among the least known authors are Boehme's description of Sophia; Madathanus; and the Catholic writers: St Epiphanius, St Ambrose, St Bonaventure; St Bernard, Mary of Agreda, Anne Catherine Emmerich, M. Olier; and scores of others who have been admirably inspired!

sublime amalgamation is impossible, so let us separate some of the elements.

The daughter of Joachim and Anne was beautiful. She possessed an intimate and touching beauty through the inner glow that permeated her countenance with the intensity of expression that often harmonizes irregular features, lighting them from within like a sanctuary lamp that awakens mysterious restlessness in the passerby.

Nicephorus Callistus, a writer in the 14th century, quoting St Epiphanius, who wrote in the 4th century, says that the Virgin was a little taller than average; her complexion had warm ivory tones; she had blond hair, bright eyes with olive-green pupils; her nose was rather long, her face oval, her fingers and hands long and slender. Rather accessible and affable, yet simple, humble, and of few words.

Do you find this sketch revealing? Does it not permit you to visualize the tall, draped silhouette of Mary, descending the stepped alleys of the little white village on her way to the fountain or the mill, kindly urging the little donkey with soulful eyes. Can you see her in the evening busily engaged in her backyard, active and silent, compassionate towards adults, smiling at the children, her eyes filled to the brim with the delights of the dawn and the magnificence of the setting sun? Cloistered in the Temple since the age of three, she came out to become engaged at fourteen at a time corresponding to the beginning of our month of September. Six months later, towards the end of March, the visitation of the angel took place. Mary left soon after, to visit her cousin Elizabeth, whom she attended at the birth of the Precursor on June 24, according to tradition. She returned to Nazareth during the first week of July.

The Virgin

The Virgin's life was always a simple one. She took care of her home, lived the life of an ordinary housewife. All her free hours were spent in prayer, which she often said during what should have been her sleeping hours. As any Israelite, she often thought of the Messiah and anxiously awaited his coming. But I must mention here something incomprehensible and unusual in her regard. Before the angel's visitation, she new nothing of her role. And after the visit, which she did not understand, a veil descended upon her mind. She remained perplexed. She saw her child born, grow, and act, without seeing. Even the miracles of her Son did not open her eyes. It seems that she had to live in this frightful blindness in order to justify in advance these sovereign words: "Woman, what is there common between you and me?" And also: "Who is my mother, who are my brothers and sisters?" It was as if this unique family, the holy family, had to keep within its breast the most glacial disunited breath and the most insurmountable incomprehension. What mortal melancholy formed the basis of this woman's existence! What perpetual sorrow for the archsensitive heart of the God-child!

How startling must be the force of ignorance and of silence, for the Word to have judged such hard precautionary measures indispensable to his work? What a lesson for our curiosity, and for our vanity in being shrewd! How that leads us towards the humble stages of spiritual poverty! How that teaches us defiance against being self-opinionated!

Yet Mary knew the Scriptures. She knew her lineage, her vow of virginity. She witnessed miracles; she heard all about her Son; she saw him die. And yet, nothing was revealed to her. Victorious ignorance overwhelms her. Her earthly conscience does not recognize him whom her divine soul loves and desires since the beginning of time. A psychologist's mind falters before this formidable blindness. Yet the voices of tradition, the teaching of the Councils, and the direct vision that is the privilege of the Friends of God are unanimous in affirming that she truly was the mother of Jesus Christ as man and as God.

We will not mention the naturalistic or materialistic hypotheses, nor the thousands of rather puerile details that the ecstatics give us. It is sufficient for us to see in the Virgin the perfection of womanhood. She has undergone all of their pains: a lonely childhood, a premature marriage (which was ill-assorted according to common sense), perpetual poverty, a poignant maternity, the constant worry for her daily bread during her lifetime, and in her old age widowhood and the loss of her beloved Son.

Heed, you girls, women, wives, and mothers: because she has shared all your pains, she will always extend her compassion to you. It is for you she has languished, it is for you she obeyed social dictates, bowed to tedious customs, and to bothersome neighbors. It is for you she accepted to be united to an elderly, impecunious spouse; it is for you she brought up a child, adored above all others, one whom she felt to be so distant, and so different. It is for you she met the problem of feeding her family, of finding the next day's lodging. It is for you she suffered the agonies brought on by the hatred and anger this Son awakened as he flaunted established concepts, as he went against preconceived opinions. Finally, it is for you she accompanied him after the betrayal with vacant eyes, and witnessed his falls, counted his wounds, listened to his moans, and was present at the last throes of his agonizing death. Almost driven mad by that most frightful grief, she cast a desperate anguished eye

The Virgin

towards the closed heavens, yet keeping her faith intact, in complete humility with a prayer on her lips.

Women, you who complain because a servant breaks a dish, you who nag a husband and children, who exploit a dressmaker without qualms, who tear a friend's reputation to shreds in order to feed your vanity; you, women who waste hours in church bringing back nothing but venom for your slander; you, vulnerable women, snobbish women who prize both title and fortune that destiny granted you freely; you, so-called virtuous women, lower than the adulteress; you, women who still live debauched lives in spite of your decaying bodies; it is for you all, for each of you personally, that the Virgin kept house alone, without servants; that she wove her own linen and woolen garments; that she never had but one dress; that she lived in silence; that she deprived herself the consolation of attending Temple worship; that she, daughter of kings, lived as a seamstress; that she fasted, prayed, and kept vigil.

Will you not do something for her? Will you not control yourselves when the occasion arises, in gratitude to her who endured all this for you over two thousand years ago?

Of course the soul of the Virgin had incarnated on earth many times before. Of course she had experienced and learned all things. But her last incarnation was like the concentrated synthesis of all her prior works. That is why she exerts over humankind, specially upon women, a perpetual ministry of assistance and of surveillance.

History does not mention her inner crises, yet they were violent—though not as the ascetic writers claim. I repeat that her terrestrial personality was unaware that the messianic drama was being enacted right there through her and under her eyes. She suffered only what any other perfect mother would have suffered in her place. Her conscience did not have to directly undergo the repercussions of the pains of her Son or the attacks of the Adversary. It is upon her inner spirit that the depredations and martyrdoms were exerted. Her terrestrial mentality only felt its whiplash. Whether counted as seven in the old German liturgies, or as five, as St Dominic did for the rosary, her joys and sorrows were dramas played only in the superhuman regions of her self.[2] That is how the faithful, when reciting the rosary with a pious heart, can really climb in spirit up to the sublime sojourns where resides the eternal Virgin, the Wisdom of the Father.

One must not conclude from what we have said that the Virgin was merely the inert instrument of messianic designs. Her life had spiritual influence. Her spirit worked on an entirely different plane, but in a manner parallel to the activity of her Son. In order to understand it, let us try to penetrate with all necessary respect the very soul of this woman, justly magnified among all others.

⊕

The life of the Absolute, the beings that fill it, the activities deployed in it, the phenomena that unfold in it—all of it together equals: the Word. The eternal Virgin is like the

---

[2] There are five *joyous* mysteries: the Annunciation, the Visitation, the Nativity, the Presentation, and Jesus at the Temple. There are five *dolorous* mysteries: the Agony, the Scourging, the Crowning with Thorns, the Carrying of the Cross, and the Crucifixion. There are five *glorious* mysteries: the Resurrection, the Ascension, Pentecost, the Assumption, and the Crowning. The first are commemorated on Mondays and Thursdays; the second on Tuesdays and Fridays; the third on Wednesday, Saturday, and Sundays. Someday we will investigate the hidden secrets of these liturgies.

The Virgin

atmosphere, the envelope, the very substance of this kingdom. Up there with all the plenitude and perfection peculiar to this world of the Presence and of Reality, she is the servant of the Lord. He and She preexist Creation. They are, if I dare say it, coeternal, and their life is to incarnate, in their person, the commands of the Father. Thus do they both increase—the Word giving life to Wisdom, Wisdom nourishing the Word. They develop constantly, totally, and endlessly.

Each created soul is a spark of the Word, clothed with a breath of the celestial Virgin. That is why beings *clamor* for heaven. Yet no matter what we may say, whatever the greatest geniuses may relate of their ecstasies, the Virgin and Christ will ever and always remain incomprehensible to man, even those who may have become as splendid and as great as gods. It will be only from the hour when the Spirit will pour his last and definitive baptism upon the restored simplicity of our heart that we will perceive the veritable dawn over the eternal shores.

The name Mary comes from a root that, according to the Hebraic scholars, signifies "to be strong" or "to be a rebel." According to the philologists, the mystical etymologies of the name are false. For us, on the contrary, they are the most likely. When St Bonaventure teaches that Mary means "bitterness, illuminatrix, or mistress"; when Boehme sees in it, in what he calls the language of nature, "the salvation in the valley of tears"; and when others find therein purified affliction or exalted purification,[3] all these visionaries open

---

[3] According to the Brahmanic codes, this name corresponds to 13 and 11 and to the astrological sign of Scorpio, which immediately brings to mind the serpent of Genesis. Kabbalistically, we find in it the universal waters—Maim—particularized by R, the sign of actual existence, etc.

the door to intuitions that are often quite direct. The number attributed to it mystically, the seven or seventy, is the number of consummation, of expiation, of exile.[4] Terrestrially, the Virgin is a synthesis of universal dolor.

Before the worlds were, before the sounding of the deep, before the elevation of the firmament, the Father contemplated himself in uncreated Wisdom—the one that is divine space and the place of the center of all things. This Wisdom—queen of angels and men, mirror of the Trinity, the bride sung by the magi-king, form and measure of Truth, abode of the Holy Spirit (with whom some agnostics assimilated her erroneously) remains forever the collaboratrix of her Creator, who consults with her and heeds her. In one of her functions she is manifesting nature, in another she celebrates the ultimate mysteries in man, in a third she realized and gave a body to the redeeming design of the Father; in a fourth she gathers the supplications of all creatures. And then, she distributes help, accompanies beings from their trespasses to their rebirth, and, finally, intercedes for one and all on Judgment Day.

Such are the septenary works of the Virgin.

Before the eternal light can be definitely relit in the temple of our heart, before the birth of Christ can take place, the self, transmuted, must become a virgin, similar to the Virgin triumphant over the serpent. We must undo the evil committed, sacrifice ourselves, keep mum, suffer, humble ourselves, impoverish ourselves, learn how to pray. These are the kindergarten classes we must attend beforehand. Only then will our personality become as clear as the walls

---

[4] Cf. Alcuin, Amalarius, Yves of Chartres.

The Virgin

of the celestial Jerusalem, our will become as strong as the tower of David, as the ivory tower, or the house of gold spoken of in the litanies. Only then will our intellect become the throne of wisdom.

As the Holy Spirit prepared both the body and soul of Mary in order to forge them into a link between heaven and earth, he too prepares the self within us, so that the light may descend directly into our physical life, enabling it from there to radiate upon the material world. At last the magnificent mystical rose promised the Bridegroom will bloom on this stem of the self—the rose all sages have foreseen, all prophets have extolled.

But if we reconsider, beyond ourselves, the dual spirit of the Virgin, both terrestrial and celestial, we discover her to be the intermediary par excellence between man and God. Never does her Son refuse her a favor. Even the graces she has not personally asked for pass through her hands. Truthfully, the Our Father and the Hail Mary should suffice us. These two formulas contain all ideas, all powers, and all our needs.

In the invisible plane that is the center of the omniverse—the colony of eternity—the gigantic spirit of the Virgin is really seen as the road of roads, the path that leads to Christ, the gate of heaven—in short, the Ark of the Covenant, where the dual promises of God to human beings, and of the Word to each of us, repose.

When in the darkest night of the soul, when a cry of anguish tears the darkness, when the Bridegroom surges forth suddenly and our heart swoons in an unchecked surge at his sight, the Virgin is there, preparing the banquet and presiding at the spiritual union of the creature and the Creator. The enclosed garden opens. From the fountain, until then sealed, the water of eternal life suddenly gushes forth.

Such is the role of the Virgin in the great saga of regeneration. It is the one where we see her best, the least confusedly. Her other activities still remain very difficult for the majority of us to decipher.

⊕

A sanctuary had to be chosen for the soul, the mind, the personality, and the physical bodies of Jesus—a sanctuary where all of these divine organisms and radiant substances could be developed in the vicinity of this formidable power without causing suffering to any of the poor and impure forms of terrestrial life. Also, it had to be done without any of the followers of the Adversary being aware of the gestation of these redeeming marvels.

That is why the chosen Virgin had to be the most humble among women. Humility forges the most impenetrable shield for the one who practices it.

This is also why this Virgin was purity itself. Before descending among us for this last mission, she had been baptized by the Holy Spirit—the baptism that redeems unto the last vestige of evil. Her spirit was pure when it came as a link between Joachim and Anne. It remained pure, even from the slightest harmless, illicit thought until her departure, when, in that blessed moment of ascension to receive the crown, she dropped her belt at St Thomas's feet. The Church was in concord with the invisible realities when it proclaimed the Immaculate Conception. The Fathers, from St Jerome onward, had mentioned this unique privilege to which the Koran itself also calls attention. The Virgin Mother is a true and universal tradition.

The Virgin

The women who gave birth to Krishna, Gautama, and other pre-messianic saviors remained immune from any human impregnation. The fathers of these children, however were gods but not God, spirits but not the Spirit.

It was necessary that the mother of the Lord reunite within the depths of her mentality the innocence of the law of nature and the rigors of the law of Moses, so as to prove that she was the living fulfillment of promises and prophecies. She had to fully comply with the law, otherwise she would have prevented the descent of the Messiah. The praise that the Church awards her, in her office as the Immaculate Conception,[5] as having been chosen from the beginning of time, is not sufficient. Each creature has been chosen since the beginning. But the other laws: "Joy of Angels" and "Abode of God" are exact and worthy of her.

Because Mary heads a series of unique privileges in past, present, and future humanity, the Church awards to her a particular cult—that of hyperdulia. During the liturgical year, she devotes numerous feast days, three months out of twelve, and one day a week, to the Virgin. Outside of the great solemn feasts known to all, let us note the feast day of Our Lady of Good Counsel, April 26, when the Church identifies her expressly as "seat of Eternal Wisdom." There is a hymn that states: "Mother of love, of fear, of conscience, and of hope, in me the grace of the way, and of truth, hope in life, and virtue are contained"! Liturgy also declares the Virgin to be the supreme refuge of sinners and of Christians, in a feast day commemorating the victorious battle of Lepante; and that she is a thaumaturgist under the name of Our Lady of Mount Carmel. Finally, there are

---

[5] Dating from 1679. Pius IX defined the doctrine solemnly in 1854.

innumerable texts where she is praised as mediatrix, refuge, advocate, and auxiliatrix at the hour of death.

Just as the month of December is consecrated to the awaited Messiah, January to the Childhood of Jesus, and February to the Holy Face, the month of March recapitulates the famous dates of the mystical history of the world. According to Catholic tradition, on March 25, the world was created, Abel was killed, St Michael vanquished Satan, Adam was buried on Golgotha, Melchizedek offered the bread and wine, and Abraham wanted to sacrifice his son Isaac. On March 25, the Annunciation took place, and it will be the end of the world. Among the Hebrews and Romans, it was the first month of the year.

May, however, is the month that belongs to Mary in her ministry, as refuge of souls and of bodies, and as sower of the benediction of nature. The month of August, month of her glory, is dedicated to her as protector of France; August starts under the sign of the Lion of Judah and ends under the sign of Virgo, the latter governing the first twenty days of September, when the Church commemorates the colors of Mary. Lastly, in the week, Saturday (day of Saturn)—sadness, humility, ordeals, meditation, and penance—is consecrated to her.

Here I must particularly mention the *Angelic Salutation*. After the *Pater Noster*, this prayer is the most powerful in all Christianity—and, I might add, among all religions. It is the result of the collaboration of an angel with diverse personages and it unites us with the first among creatures; just as the Lord's Prayer, which unites us to the Father, was given to us by the Son.

The Angelic Salutation is composed of three parts:

The Virgin

(1) The words of Gabriel: "Hail Mary, full of grace, the Lord is with thee."

(2) The salutation with which Elizabeth welcomed her cousin: "Thou art blessed among all women, and blessed is the fruit of thy womb, Jesus."

(3) The invocation: "Holy Mary, Mother of God, pray for us, poor sinners, now, and at the hour of our death. Amen."

The first two parts are of ancient usage in the Church. They are to be found textually, or under an equivalent form, in the liturgy of St James the Lesser and in the *Antiphon* of St Gregory the Great. According to Baronius and Bona, the third part is due to the Council of Ephesus in AD 431. The *Hail Mary* is to be found in the manual of prayers of a patriarch of Alexandria in the 7th century, except for the last words, "now and at the hour of our death," which are more recent and seem to have been added by the Franciscans. This prayer was introduced in France by Louis VI. Cromwell forbade it in England at the time when Louis XIII consecrated his kingdom to the Virgin.[6]

The *Angelus*, which has been recited three times a day since the time of Urban II, is based upon the *Angelic Salutation*. It is composed of three verses, quoting exactly the words of the angel, the answer of Mary, and the Incarnation; an *Ave Maria* follows each one of the verses, and it ends in a prayer. We note again the number seven—the number of the Virgin. The final oremus may be translated thus: "We implore you to shed your grace into our souls

---

[6] It is easy to partition the Latin or French texts of this prayer so as to bring out the kabbalistic, alchemistic, or subjective meanings.

(*mentibus*) so that, having known of the incarnation of Jesus Christ by the voice of the angel, we might through his Passion reach the glory of his Resurrection." By a remarkable coincidence, the sequence of this ascetic pursuit is clearly indicated by the Protestant Jacob Boehme and by the Rosicrucians of 1604 (Protestants also).

Let us notice that the *Angelus* must be recited while kneeling during the week, and while standing on Sundays; doubtless, because on the day of the Lord, his astronomical representative—the sun—functions especially in the invisible and finds itself in a special correspondence with the mysterious forces that brought the pure substance of the body of Christ into the womb of the Virgin. Let us now consider what we may know of the effects and ends of this mysterious prayer.

⊕

There is between the earth and other planets, especially between the earth and the sun, an exchange of forces. These currents are subject to the analogous laws that rule magnetism and electricity and that regularly modify their polarity. At each passage from one tension to the other, there is a slight pause, an emptiness that occurs in the moving enormity—at each period of the mentioned circuit, their polarity changes. In the Platonic year there are four of these periods, each of 6000 years, separated one from the other by a particular cataclysm on the physical plane and by a judgment on the spiritual plane. There Christ sits as judge and his Mother as intercessor.

In the common year, those four periods are the seasons, each separated by the two equinoxes and two solstices. These four epochs must evidently possess special proper-

The Virgin

ties, since all religions recognize them by feasts and important ceremonies.

As for the day, sunrise and sunset, noon and midnight, are the times when the changes of polarity occur.

In each of the "stops" of this triple series, please recall your attention to the fact that there occurs an upheaval of forces and of souls, human and otherwise, and that there is there a presence or an influence of the Word and of the Virgin. Since nature has a horror of a vacuum, as soon as there is an emptiness, it is instantly filled with a force of an immediately superior degree. The religious man who knows that his prayers do not reach heaven in an instant, but that they ascend degree by degree towards the higher and higher inner spheres, takes advantage of formulating his prayer at the instant when one of these vacuums occurs. Because this void propagates to higher and more subtle planes, these successive aspirations carry along with them the prayer, which is substance and force—and so the faithful have many more chances of being heard. The natural phenomenon utilized by the Hindu for his *Sandhyas* is utilized by the Catholic for his *Angelus*.

In this way the Virgin is shown under the new aspect of queen of the fluidic or etheric forces, which is one of the interpretations of her sacred title: star of the sea. These are some of the general ideas I meant to convey to you, hoping that the intuition you feel in your heart regarding the personality and the role of the Virgin Mary enables you to see that in reality there are not two Precursors of Christ as I stated before, but three.

In fact, if the just men and the patriarchs were preparing the obvious life of our planet to receive the divine visit, then, while John the Baptist was laying the foundations

THE CHILDHOOD OF JESUS

needed for the secret life (preparing the spiritual armies and his contemporaries according to the regimen of penitent expiation), the Virgin was erecting the temple, adorning it, purifying it, and holding it in readiness for him. She performed this majestic work not only in the cosmos and on earth but also within the hearts of the believer torn by tears of repentance.

Let us have this triple horizon ever-present in our mind; and, at least, if we are not able to realize absolute abnegation in current practice, let us attempt to reach it for a few moments once in a while, because the self has need of varied medicines. If you have done this with all sincerity in your search for truth, someday you will be surprised to find yourself at the eve of a complete transformation.

The Trinity

MONG ALL the portraits of himself that the Absolute has offered to man, the highest and most living is the Christian Trinity. Believe this, till some day when I will attempt to dissect the syntheses of the Brahmans, Taoists, Kabbalists, or of the Pythagoreans for those of you who are interested in these things. They bear but a superficial resemblance to each other, as each, true to its own end, is a special world and the center of a world; the terms of each are alive from a mode proper to created life, and from an individual reflection of absolute life.

Let us be satisfied to know that God—him from whom all things come—is the Father; that God—by whom all subsists—is the Son; and that God—in whom all harmonizes—is the Spirit.

The Father is power, immobility, unity, creation.
The Son is wisdom, beauty, motion, generation.
The Holy Spirit is love, truth, concord, union.

There is a mysterious relationship between the spirit of man and the Spirit of God. The Spirit joins by a continuous procession the innumerable simultaneous wills of the Cause of causes, who is the Father, to the innumerable successive phenomena of universal life that are the acts of the Son.

By another continuous procession, the spirit of man joins the eternal soul (the permanent principle of our being) to all the operations of the self that mold our personal life. It is upon this spirit that the Holy Spirit descends first. It is this spirit that first receives from the Holy Spirit advice and consolation. It is for this spirit that the Paraclete intercedes and pleads, and that he accompanies the self, instructing and encouraging it. Just as the Holy Spirit is the love of the Father for the Son, and that of the Son for the Father, so is the spirit of man the dual love of the soul and of the self. Just as the Holy Spirit after his descent (which followed that of Christ) reascends to the Father, taking along with him the universal concert of creatures, so the spirit of man, after having brought to the self the light of the soul, brings back to the soul the essence of all the efforts of the self.

The Holy Spirit, Freedom, and Truth are one and the same substance. By it alone may increase, in the unknowable center of the conscious being, the germ of free will that the Father loaned it since the beginning. Only through the Spirit can the intellect grasp the truth—the infinitely fleeting sixfold relationship of the objects to be perceived with the organs of perception and with the intermediating surroundings.

That is why Jesus promises beatitude to the poor in spirit. For they alone, knowing how not to become proud of their natural gifts, may receive supernatural plenitudes. They alone, standing naked before glory, may clothe themselves with the inconceivable virtues of the Paraclete as just so many brilliant robes. They alone, accustomed to the startling darknesses of faith, perceive unaltered the true forms of creatures. They alone, the poor in spirit, possess omniscience, omnipotence, and beatitude.

The Trinity

It is through the Spirit, faithful messenger of the Father and of the Son, that our intellect, "assumed" to the eternal present, reviews the past, penetrates the future, and prophesies. It is by the Spirit that the disciple drives the demons away, heals the sick, remits sins, turns catastrophes away, hears the language of the dumb and of invisible creatures, and makes himself understood by them. It is by the Spirit that the knowledge of God and of Jesus grows in us. It is the Spirit who causes prayer to gush from those hard rocks of our heart.

The Spirit liberates us three ways: by living knowledge, he dissipates the multiform illusions of the senses; by having our prayers answered, he liberates us from the illusion of force; by engendering in us love, he breaks the chains of the law. Without the Spirit, we would obey only out of fear of justice, or covetousness for recompense. With the Spirit, we obey through love; or rather, we do not *obey* any more, we *live* in God—we anticipate his orders, we labor in the pure swoon of unity.

According to the theologians, the Spirit communicates himself by seven modes, but none have ever defined these gifts—probably because none have yet received them wholly. The are called wisdom, intelligence, counsel, force, science, pity, and the fear of God—words interchangeable to our blindness. The wise doctors explain them as best they can. We must be thankful to divine kindness for our ignorance, because were we to know the Spirit, we could offend him, and we would be lost. All I may say regarding the supernatural seedings planted by Jesus in this land-of-the-living (of whose existence in the center of ourselves we know nothing) is that they grow silently when and if our bad conduct does not smother them, and that they lead us to the total transformation of our being, up to and including our body. When God alone lives within us, our actions are their fruits. That is why natural laws then comply with our prayers, veils fall, and all creatures answer and obey.

Elsewhere I have shown that the marvels of ancient esotericisms are but the artificial counterparts of Christic miracles.

Let us visualize the Father, immutable in the bosom of his eternity. Let us visualize the prodigious descent of the Son through the zodiacs and innumerable spheres, from the ecstatic angels and gods on their knees, to the adoration of unknown races, to the terror of stupefied demons. Let us also visualize the Spirit who followed the Son, how his subtle wake becomes wider and deeper in proportion to the new martyrdoms that Jesus accepts as he gives more affirmative testimonies on many other lands.

Collectively, the manifestation of the Spirit remains progressive. It comes of a sudden only to exceptional beings. The human personality receives all it can absorb—an overbrimming and overflowing amount, yet so small in comparison to what it will be in the Kingdom. The Virgin, Zacharias, Elizabeth, John the Baptist, the apostles, the disciples, even some pagans, have been "filled" with it. And in the last days, after the great upheavals, the Consoler will visit "each body of flesh" to prepare it for the glories of authentic regeneration. And by his very secret influence, the visible and invisible disciples, along with their companion collaborators, will combine to form but one body and one spirit.

The Spirit is alive. He passes into a heart, over a thing, within a social body, leaving therein a lasting perfume—he flows into it continuously and fills all surroundings. For

The Trinity

example, look at our old France (if you are too young to have known its ancient peoples, read Michelet, who, though an inaccurate historian—partial and visionary according to modern schools—was yet French to the core).

We were all profoundly Christians once upon a time. There is a lot more Christianity in Villon and in Bayle, among the Encyclopedists, than among the actual members of the *Action Francaise*. The characteristics of the French were to be patient, thrifty, deliberate, and happy. Where is the factory worker today who sings on his way to work? Wages were ridiculously low—yet still, one brought up children. There were no cars, no vaudevilles, no department stores; a man liked his work. The idea of sabotage would not have entered the mind of these workmen. To damage a tool, to waste raw materials, would have seemed pure folly to them. Their labor was honor itself.

From this honor was born their common sense, their courage, frankness, their respect for womanhood, for old people, for the child, their veneration for the home. Their whole life, their profession, work, meals, baptism and catechism, engagements and funerals, the town's feasts and the daily exchanges among neighbors, were based upon tradition, legacies, unwritten laws—which were all French, all Christic. Yes, admittedly French sons of the Celts, of Gaul, and of Rome; but all Christians just the same—sons of the Son of the Carpenter.

All of this was the work of the Spirit, a work that, interrupted for the past fifty years, seems to have sunk body and soul into the actual tempest, but which we trust our grandchildren will see reborn.

THE CHILDHOOD OF JESUS

⊕

With loving kindness and careful tenderness, Christ gives us the pledge of our beatitude and of our future liberty. His Spirit surrounds us in a thousand ways. It is in order not to dazzle us that he hides behind the phosphorescent phantoms of science, of art, and of thought, whose splendor is nothing but a smoky dawn to the magnificent mornings over the eternal hills.

Of course, there is a progressive illumination in all modes of our terrestrial life, owing to the evolutive power given to all beings from their creation. But we cannot surpass our limit. Also, we make mistakes. Were inflexible justice alone to rule, we would be bound to endless returns, so as to take up our botched-up works again, to find the right path and rectify our depredations. But Jesus, his Mother, and the Spirit intercede with their supernatural mercies, which are divine, extraordinary, free, infinitely rich, precise, and varied.

When the Consoler takes over a man and crowns him as herald of intelligence or ambassador of beauty, we call it genius. When he finds a heart burning with the desire for God, he quenches that heart's thirst at the eternal spring, and that is called sanctity. The saint and the genius breathe the same breaths, but they assimilate them differently.

Both are unclassifiable, unexpected, illogical, and the essential fruits of their efforts unpredictable. So: even as the total Word incarnated into the womb of the Virgin "by the operations of the Holy Spirit," the ulterior and fragmentary sparks of this Word have reincarnated since, are incarnating, and will always incarnate by just as many special operations of the same divine Spirit.

Such are the principal testimonies of the Spirit. The Son

The Trinity

gives witness to the Father. The Spirit gives witness to the Father. The Spirit gives witness to the Son. Blood and water give witness to the Spirit. Water represents all this immense nature built by the Son. It is also the Virgin Mother. Blood is universal suffering, which as a vassal bows at the feet of the only innocent Martyr. And the concert of these reciprocal testimonies organize all along what we call duration of time, the harmony wherein on the last day the now concordant clamors of the worlds and their inhabitants will be resolved.

⊕

How can we attempt to reduce these grand perspectives and use them in our little daily life? Prayer alone gives us the means.

It is the Paraclete within us who implores "by ineffable sighs." It is he, the secret adorer, through whom pure prayer ascends—silent, though our voice accompanies it; spontaneous, though we must force the self to its knees; free, though pain constrains us; beautiful, though we are still mean. How does one express the arcana of prayer? And if it were possible, should I reveal it?

Adoration in spirit is the free prostration of love. Adoration in truth is by the fervor of our fatigues. The gold, myrrh, and incense that the child Jesus lying in the manger of the self accepts with a smile as he presents them to the Father are our mumbling mouth, our weary hands, and arid heart.

Rites remain but symbols if they are not nourished by works and animated by love. The mystical bread and wine alone communicate their vigor to liturgies, making them capable of taking our soul up to the gate of glory. If done without ascetic effort and without obedience to duty, the use of sacraments is a triple sin: the sin of laziness, of hypocrisy, and of profanation. It is an insult to divine succor! And how many people are not guilty of these unworthy and illusive expedients?

The most complete and sound among the various religions is Christianity. And among the Christian religions, Catholicism, although we must admit that no church is what it should be. The Greek Church suffers from apathy. The Protestant Church is becoming sterile by the abuse of exegesis and "free-thinking." And as for the Catholic Church, St Hildegard, St Bernard. St Catherine of Sienna, St Vincent de Paul, the Cure d'Ars, and how many others have wept over her faults. Parasitic devotions are invading her more and more. The vices of propaganda and of success are poisoning her. And how much more I could say...!

But it is better that I remember the very patient Gardener who does not shatter the half-broken reed. Let us put polemics, controversies, and apologetics aside. Jesus does not need lecturers, or professors. He only wants apostles and workers for his vineyard. Yes, let us express our beliefs, but more so, let us live them. In the measure wherein we will make our truth identical to Truth, so will our truth be able to defend itself alone, and will triumph.

If we notice in someone a preference, or even a slight tendency towards a particular religious expression, it means that for this person it is better than the austere religion of the Spirit. Moreover, the religion of the Spirit appears arid only to those who do not enter into it. We must guide people towards what seems good to them. We must explain the cult they desire, making it possible for them to discover God therein. Especially, we must make them understand

The Trinity

that, in the spiritual, one cannot walk on two paths at the same time. In order to benefit from a certain light, one must enter body and soul into the ranks it illumines. It is impossible to be at the same time Catholic and Protestant, Catholic and Spiritualist, Catholic and Theosophist. One must choose. If one decides for Catholicism, one must accept all that the Church orders and renounce all that she forbids. Otherwise, one loses the benefit of the two or three spiritual collectivities from which one hoped to profit.

But, I repeat, the worst error of a great number of Christians is to believe themselves to be Christians, that because they attend Mass regularly—though without giving up slander, without overcoming their avariciousness, their ruse and hardness towards little people, their vanity and social climbing—they are Christians! The Church is big enough and strong enough for her sons to accept such criticisms without loving her less. And, if she declares prayer and the use of sacraments to be indispensable, yet does she not repeat with sufficient force that not to trouble oneself, to forget the unfortunate, to make up for this laziness by attending divine services, is but hypocrisy? To ask God for a happy fortune without wanting to take the necessary trouble—would that not be imposing on him to be an accomplice to our laziness? "Heaven helps him who helps himself."

Between an unbeliever who lives honestly and wears himself out helping others, and the scrupulously devout man who buries himself in selfish comfort and heartless pride, it is the unbeliever who is the better Christian—because Jesus preached above all else action, and did so *by* his actions. Active works are indispensable. Faith alone only serves as preparation. On every page, the gospel proclaims the indispensable necessity of actions. Your duty is to impart this, and especially to exemplify it.

As for those who do not feel the need for rites, Christ will not condemn them, provided they perform the precepts of charity, that they do not consider themselves superior to the churchgoers, that they labor for heaven alone. If such is your opinion, be wise enough not to discourage others from attending the liturgies they like and from which they receive help. Have the dual ardor of serving God first because of what each Christian owes him and for what you too owe him because of your title as friends of his Son. That is a heavy title to bear, especially when you realize that Jesus often confers it upon you by anticipation. It is a terrible responsibility that comes your way: you find yourself upon a stage whence your acts and feelings resound much farther than you had ever imagined.

Whether you want to or not, you radiate by the mere fact that you belong to Jesus. But do not try to become conscious of that influence. Apply your energy only to the task of making yourself more docile for the work that the Master is preparing for you. We are by nature animals that at times are either ferocious or slinking. We must tame ourselves. It is the only work God asks—or rather, demands—of us, and if we do not apply ourselves willingly, he has a thousand means of inclining us to do so.

This tyranny and violence upon one's self are necessary in order for us to become disciples. A disciple must understand everything, forgive everything, accept everything, and fall in with everything. He has the right to keep silent about his inner life. "My secret belongs to me," St Theresa used to say. But the disciple must take care to never scandalize the innocent souls who are so precious to the Virgin,

The Trinity

those who do not separate religion from its cultural forms, who do not perceive the true kernel within so many pious sermons, and who do not comprehend that God may hear us without the help of priests.

The disciple adheres strictly to the maxim: "Judge not...!" He denies himself any form of criticism: he must even deny himself the unexpressed feeling of blame. He must obey, as his Master did before him, all laws and customs in order to master himself. He must learn obedience and even surpass obedience. Just as he submits to civil laws, he goes to Mass, has his children baptized in order not to cause scandal, and not "to snuff out the wick that is still smoldering." Maybe the humble prayer of the disciple, molded in the rigid form of rite, will reawaken and reanimate within himself the ardor that once upon a time exalted him. Nothing disappears from this earth—not a being, not an idea, not an institution—until it has reached its full career: not until it has exhausted the patience of justice or the tender solicitude of mercy.

So, even though you may not see the possible sophistications of Christ's maxims, never blame the priests. Most of them are crushed under the heavy load of their sacerdotal office. The Adversary erects his most powerful batteries against them, and lays subtle traps beneath their feet. The priests shoulder a frightful responsibility. Do not judge them. Rather, admire the zeal of a few among them. And if you do not believe their ministry useful to you, at least try to make your zeal superior to theirs, and then measure to see if yours even equals theirs.

It is easy to say that Mass and Confession are good for the people who do not know how to reach God without an intermediary. Yes, perhaps, but you—do you reach God, who is so close to you? Let us become humble. Pride exudes from all our pores, so let us throw ourselves into the inner precipices of humility. We must feel very small, very naked, and most unworthy in order for the Consoler to descend.

So, if anyone speaks to you of the Church, of priests, of devotions, limit your answers to the three principles upon which all theologians agree, and which Jesus has proclaimed: believe, help the poor, pray. Keep on repeating that Jesus loves us, that his one desire is to win our love, and that this beatitude is offered to all. Carry the load of the weak, reawaken the lukewarm, re-establish harmony around you, avoid any words that might create distrust. Your task is not to make others work, but to work for others—as Jesus does for us and for all.

Jesus did not spare harsh reproaches to the priests of his day. He could, alas! repeat them today. But you are nothing but disciples—tiny little ones. You do not even know the alphabet of the Book of Life. To criticize is not your concern. Take stock of your nothingness. The good you do... it is not you, it is Jesus who accomplishes it through you. Our most rigid fights against vices, our most desperate strifes against selfishness, are nothing but the outcry of our goodwill shrieking to God. Look at the saints and at all those who relit the dying flame of the mystic torch from their own substance: they were men who possessed a formidable will, and yet all believed themselves to be ignorant and powerless.

Close your eyes to evil. Open them to see nothing but good. Fill them with the splendors of beauty instead of searching for something to be criticized. Search for noble actions so that you may praise them—for no matter how mean the world may be, noble actions are not lacking. May

The Trinity

your intelligence, your sensitivity, and your love welcome all that comes to you: but weigh everything in the scales of the Spirit.

The Master of the field permits the weeds and the wheat to grow side by side: it is not man but other beings who harvest. Concern yourself only with the ripening of the wheat. As the Father gives his life, his sunlight, his joy to all, give also to all what they ask you for above all, in spite of their apparent demands. By this I mean: fraternal help plus affectionate exhortations towards the ineffable certitudes you have received.

To receive the imperceptible "seed" of eternity, which is more precious than all suns, flesh and nature must be ploughed down to their entrails. Man must submit to the plowshare of sorrow in a state of unknowing, because unknowing engenders faith, and faith is such an extraordinary thing that no scholar has yet been able to explain it. Let us say that it is the force by which the Father orders the world to be. Within us, faith is the virtue of the Father, just as love is the virtue of the Son, hope is the virtue of the Holy Spirit, and humility is the virtue of the Virgin.

What prodigious beings we will be when a bit of faith will live in us! Everything will be possible for us on earth. We will become its gods, but we won't be aware of it, as blissful ignorance will still be there to save us from satanic pride.

This world, the human species, and nature—these are the raw materials, one and triple, of an immense transmutation—the *grand-oeuvre*, the "great work"—of which the Son is the alchemist and the Holy Spirit the secret fire. This inert, impure, heavy matter delights in her gross state, does not wish to become radiant. However, the Son her alchemist loves her for the subtle essence hidden within her. He wants her to become splendid. He would like her to lend herself to his designs. But she resists him. She wants to wallow in her stagnation; her obstinacy condemns her to suffering because she has to evolve. And so, her Master, taking pity on her, ingeniously attempts to make her pliable.

The more she hardens, the more he loves her and wants to save her in spite of herself. He invents an admirable expedient: he descends towards her; he infuses his own vital light into her; he offers himself to the slowly devouring flames of the purifying fire he himself had lit. Thus Christ has the right of saying: "I have come to set the earth afire! Ah—how I wish it were already kindled."

Let us try to find out the mysterious mechanism of these transmutations.

That Word, consubstantial with the Spirit, equal to the Spirit, of the same nature as the Spirit, is nevertheless master of the Spirit, since it is he who gave us the promise: "I shall send you the Consoler." On the other hand, will the Spirit obey, since "He blows where he wills." That is the first contradiction.

Secondly, the Word, who is the master of the Spirit, makes himself his victim voluntarily, since he sacrifices himself through love—and that love, in God, is the Spirit.

Finally, both the master and the servant, the victim and the sacrificer, unite secretly in a most intimate collaboration in order to incite humankind to take the road of salvation.

The Trinity

Let us contemplate the startling illogicalities of the Father who wants to see his lambs return of their own free will to the fold. Jesus, who is the Father, under his guise of Shepherd, descends here-below, loaded with divine and natural treasures that he divests himself of, giving them away to all. He goes so far as to give his Mother to humankind. Already martyred upon the universal cross of the four breaths of the Holy Spirit, he finally ends upon on the cross of Golgotha. When he was imploring his Father during the silence of the nights on Galilean hills, the shadow of his raised arms prefigured the cruciform tree upon which Love was to suspend him shortly. It is for man alone that the Spirit designates himself as the Consoler. For God, the Spirit, who is Glory, champions Justice, who is the Son (the just Judge). Love, which is the Spirit, champions Wisdom, which is the creative Word of the world. Still, these two are but one; and yet the three also are but the one unique Being pre-existent to everything, independent of all, yet by compassion infused within all.

So, the Divine Persons act in the world according to modes disconcerting to our logic. Clay does not comprehend the aims of the fingers of the potter who molds it, so let us try to be intelligent clay.

During the descent of the Son throughout the worlds down to the well of Abyss, the waves of the Spirit lengthen on his trail, so that Christ can state everywhere: "My Father and I are one." At each detour of this mysterious path (which is himself) that the Word cuts open at the same time as he travels it, the wake of the Spirit extends further over a very large area—in consequence of which, no matter how far down the Savior descends, the Consoler descends still farther. And the eternal Virgin, who is the substance and atmosphere of the Kingdom, accompanies her Son the Word, and her invisible Spouse, the Spirit.

Let us consider how these voyages, these descents, these explorations (which would seem to be capricious vagrancies were we not able to see their numerous detours) cause gigantic upheavals, augment creation, extend the primal limits of the world, and reconstruct for the last day and for the last judgment a very different universe from the original one. Remember that all which is done by the Divine Persons becomes—upon all universes, all earths, upon this earth, and in each creature—a tangible, physical act that our bodily senses feel. Do we then dare fathom the infinite abasement, the dark obscurity, the immeasurable anguish woven into the terrestrial existence of the Virgin? Dare we listen to the clamors of hatred in which the crowds greet the messengers of light during their passage? And should we not expect to bear the same distress? Should we not resolve to accomplish the "obscurity of our night," to endure it all without comprehending any part of it? Should we not become so small inwardly and feel so worthless that anyone could walk over us without our hardly being aware they did?

These cruel men—spiteful Christians, stubborn Jews—they are the ones who wanted the martyrdom of the Word. They are the blind instruments of the Spirit. They are the ignominious cross. They are the tree of salvation. They are the shadow of the spirit over the shadows of hell.

They carry on still with their ferociously ironical clamor: "If you are God, come down from your cross!" But Jesus cannot come down till they are converted; and they have

The Trinity

sworn to become converted only when he comes down. What resource does the Savior possess to save them, except to annihilate himself still further, to plunge entirely into the mire of their hearts, and to effect therein, with the admirable ruse of love, the cleansing and necessary curettage, while letting them believe they are purifying themselves? This work is the very work of the Holy Spirit.

You, then, who love Jesus, who love him for himself: become the good servant of this cruel spirit of love; help him save men in spite of themselves, impel them to enter within. It is he, the rapid trapper, the vagabond hunter of souls, the ardent dog of the great shepherd who relentlessly harasses the stampeding flock, the indocile rams, and the lazy ewes. It is he, the fool, whose course no one guesses and who on the last day will push the wise ones through the frightful fog of universal confusion towards the golden gates of the promised Jerusalem, both terrestrial and divine.

Be the sheep dogs of the good shepherd. Your lot must be labors, panting errands, and cane beatings from bad farmers; scour the world unknown, unsung, muddy, worn, hungry, and in rags... all that is nothing. What is important is that on the last evening you will bring back safe and sound the flock that was put in your care.

Learn this difficult task by overcoming the faults and desires that devastate your mind. Be poor in spirit, be the "beggars" of the spirit. Must we admit that voluntary poverty, which is already so difficult, is but a luxury in our case? To become poor of one's own volition is relatively feasible. There is also the sterile poverty of the rebellious. But when in spite of ourselves our aim stretches out towards gold, when our sensitivity burns with a consuming ardor towards the enjoyment of art, when our intellect burns feverishly with thirst for knowledge, and when the perpetual Poor offers us to share his life, invites us to his terrible indigence, imposes his destitution upon us—then the most painful battle begins between the self wanting to broaden and enrich itself and the Spirit who knows of the treasure buried under mystic poverty.

Thus, the carnal self first revolts against its Lady Poverty, then accepts and even seeks her, until the Tempter comes and inoculates the self anew with covetousness—from the lowest level to the noblest. Meanwhile, angels erect an insurmountable wall between man and his desires. This is the terrible ordeal through which we all will have to pass, at the top of the mountain.

⊕

This is how divine work is wrought. Its three mysterious witnesses are there, just as St John calls them: water, spirit, and blood. Water: the immense mass of matter that the science of the engineer and the doings of the laborer transforms. Spirit: the feverish search for intelligence and all the refinements of aesthetics. Blood: all of human suffering, all the wounds and tears. And yet, even though workers are exploited by industry and international finance; even though dilettantism, scepticism, and hypocritical profit-taking prostitute the pure thirst for knowledge or the noble enthusiasm of the artist; and even though frightful ambitions cause unspeakable martyrdoms on battlefields—still, here and there, honest workers, sincere artists, and scientists who have integrity, remain. But it is the blood that, by the innumerable heroics of the servants of heaven, still gives a definite testimony of the divine character of the unknowable causes and of the mysterious reasons for actual cata-

The Trinity

clysms. Just as the Christians of the first centuries were persecuted for their Master, so also the sons of France gave back to their Mother the life they had received from her, thereby assuring by the spontaneousness of their sacrifice the most magnificent and certain future.

This is how the Spirit operates in the domain of reality. Let us now look at the Spirit operate in the speculative. Let us observe how, since the end of the seventeenth century, the various thinking activities tend to impinge upon each other.

As soon as *science* goes beyond the recording of natural phenomena and experience, it invents hypotheses, uses imagination and intuition, and enters into metaphysics.

When *philosophy* conceives the absolute as indifferent, unfeeling, and unmoving, it soon begins to doubt the truth of this conception and discovers, rather, that it is sympathetic, aesthetic, and moving, such as described by William James, Boutroux, and Henri Bergson.

Meanwhile, *art*, having codified its theory and annexed science for its technique, becomes systematized and loses its characteristic "portrayal of life" (the *allusion à la vie* of Mallarmé).

Finally, religion, or rather *theology*, attempts more and more to demonstrate with the help of science and metaphysics the exactitude of its dogmas, the truth of its mysteries, and the value of its rites.

The Latin mind, lover of order and clarity, disavows these overflowings, although they are the effervescence annunciating new modes of learning, feeling, and thinking. The Spirit operates in the midst of this frothing mass. No one discerns his work. And even much later, when the marvelous edifices of a new science, a new philosophy, or a new aesthetics will appear in full bloom, still no one will try to find the Architect who erected them.

Besides, no created form remains impervious to the Consoler, who is as wise as a serpent and as gentle as a dove. He enters everywhere. He watches all men. He takes them unawares, takes them along, carries them along. He adopts some here and there, and if he does not find the worker he needs at hand, he goes searching for him to the very ends of the zodiacs. He installs himself within his elected ones, makes them speak, predict, and pray. He submits to them the laws of distance, weight, and physiology. He sounds them out, justifies their actions, purifies them down to their roots. He unveils the celestial secrets, counteracts justice without cheating anyone, expels the demons—perhaps he even enlightens them and prepares them for salvation. Does not his wisdom seem a folly to the wisest among us?

This is because the Spirit, in his relationship with all creatures, is the multiform force itself that theologians call grace. Through his honest conduct, man may furnish himself in the universe here and there some harbors of rest, some temporary paradise. But it is impossible for him to enter into the eternal paradise, into the kingdom of God, because no creature can live in the Uncreated unless the Uncreated takes him over and reorganizes him from the bottom up. That is called the Christic regeneration, the second birth, the baptism of the Spirit.

⊕

When we aspire for heaven ardently with our whole being and above everything else, Jesus comes to meet us. The Spirit accompanies him, overshadows us, bathes us; and the mystical purifications begin. However, his mode remains

The Trinity

incomprehensible to our most scrutinizing examinations, Yes, we desire light and liberty; but light and liberty must first come to dissipate our shadows and break our chains, since we have but a partial intuitional and almost unconscious awareness of these divine figures. That is why the roads of the Spirit remain unforeseen, unexpected, and disconcerting to us: our own logic is one of servitude, wherein we languish.

The sevenfold influence of the Consoler within man penetrates to the very depths of ordinary conscience: above, below, and through it. It radiates with such subtle spontaneity that those whose forehead wears one or the other of these crowns are not even "aware" of it. Either one has not received them (the crowns) and so cannot say anything about them, or, if possessing them, one finds it impossible to speak of them because no one would understand. These splendors are equivalents in effective virtue and in dignity: they descend only upon the servants of the Father, upon the Friends, and upon the very rare soldiers of Christ—chief of the army of Light.

Their wisdom frustrates any intrigue of darkness and discerns the right solution to any conflict.

Their intelligence is that of adapting divine things to terrestrial horizons.

Their gift of counsel is that of speaking the right word to any nation, demon, man, or god as well as to a stone, and of presenting to them the assimilable light.

Their strength is that of being weak, unarmed, lacking authority, appearance, money, or friends.

Their gift of insight is their ability to see the truth about anything instantly.

Their piety is that in the slightest movement of their

body or of their spirit, in their silences as well as in their words, in their repose as well as their labors, are perpetual prayers that angels transmit and hand ever from one to another up to the chamber of the treasure of the sempiternal House.

Their fear of God is not our fear, it is love. They are obsessed by God, possessed by God: they cannot love save in God, they cannot make a gesture save through God.

But no one ever sees these things. At the most, some kind of marvel happens that opens the eyes of the sincere seekers. These slaves of the Spirit (to outward appearance, just part of the crowd) are the enclosed fountain, the secret garden, and the inviolable tower of which the magi-king speaks. Yet everyone may quench their thirst from their amphora, pick the fruit of their sagacities, and take refuge in their arms. They are the kindest of beings, since they never refuse anything to anyone; they are the most walled-in beings, because the eternal mystery that lives within them makes them undecipherable.

⊕

Remember these things when, overcome by crushing fatigue amidst terrifying perils, you will think you are nothing but miserable leaves swirling in the winds of distress. May your courage remain steadfast! You will know that these are the operations of the Spirit. You will know that such is the path of faith.

This is beyond any question of your concepts of God, of man, or of the universe. True faith will be yours when neither physical nor moral terrors can shake your confidence, when everything will spell happiness for you, when all will be clothed with the same gravity, when your eyes will discover beneath the ugliest of sights the divine face that transfigures them, when the impossible will run from your serenity, and when your very presence will give strength to the weak and stir divine disquiet within the presumptuous securities of scepticism.

You will wear these crowns, you will become such thaumaturgists only if, forgetting all marvels, you will remember to help your failing comrades and to hold out till the end. And if I show you, from time to time, the dazzling perspectives of the divine terrestrial existence of the soldiers of God, it is to enable you to give beyond your labors—in excess of the impossible—that tiny bit of energy which still remains there when you think yourselves totally drained; so that you may draw from the bottom of your being the last renunciation, accept supreme destitution and final abandonment; so that you may win pure merit—the flower of goodwill; so that, knowing how much the Father loves you, how the Son accompanies you, and with what tenderness the Spirit and the Virgin console and work along with you, you may find the strength of saying to them: "I know you love me, I know you are with me; but love me a little less and love him more, he who does not yet understand; leave me alone sometimes and go to the one who thinks he is abandoned. I will not work with less heart, I promise you; I will not complain, and I will wear upon my face the same expression of happiness that your presence is giving it at this moment."

Christ is God. Engendered by his Father from all eternity, not created as were the other beings out of chaos, he is the conscience and the knowledge which the Father takes of himself since the beginning and forever. In eternity he is one with the Father, though distinct from him. In time he is still one with the Father, though still distinct from him. Consequently, he is both the Word and the only Son. Here, as above, he lives simultaneously in the bosom of eternity as in the bosom of anterior time, ulterior duration, and the infinitesimal present. In heaven and on earth, upon all lands and in all skies, in the infinite as in our spaces, he remains the same, the sum-total of all supernatural forces, the quintessence of all that is natural, and he possesses both integral divine nature and the perfection of human nature.

Christ is above and beyond the created, independent and free from any law. At the same time, he is in the abyss of the very nature he has formed, and he submits to all the laws he has decreed. In his person all the incompatibles are assembled: he is pure spirit and perfect flesh; engendered by the eternal and born of a woman; God and man; all powerful and slave; blessed dispenser of all beatitudes and martyr of all pains; giver of life and resigned to death. Christ surpasses imagination, yet he knows how to make himself so small that his servants dare speak to him without fear.

Only one person will remain invisible forever—the Father. But he makes himself perceptible to our intelligence through his Word. Builder of all creation, he lets himself be felt by our love, through his Son. Savior of this same creation, he makes himself visible at times to our eyes through his Son Jesus Christ: our friend and master.

The Father and the Son are one. This unity is called the Spirit. Yet the Son comes from the Father, and the Spirit proceeds from the relations of the Father with the Son. The Spirit is the breath that vibrates at the command of the Word, and it is by him that humans—who carry a spark of the uncreated light—receive the divine virtues known as graces (because they are *gratis*). Isaiah the prophet enumer-

The Trinity

ates seven of the principal ones, and the Church has adopted this synthesis from her origin. But within the phalanx of the theologians, as well as within that of the mystics, few are the servants who have received the totality of those gifts. Human thought and speech are so inadequate that one is often content with the rather vague explanations, which are often divergent, on this difficult subject. However, it seems to us we could imagine it this way:

The gifts of wisdom and of intelligence, descending upon our mental faculties, would enable them to discern the truth according to God in all practical and speculative domains, and to apply this realization in each necessity of life.

The gifts of counsel and of strength, descending into our faculties of soul, would enable us to console, help, and heal as the saints and thaumaturgists do.

The gifts of science and of piety, descending upon our physical faculties, would teach us how to instill eternal light in all of our material endeavors and make us capable, by means of true prayer, of elevating all forms of terrestrial life and creatures up to God.

Finally, the gift of fear of God would come to perfect and stabilize our humility by giving us empirical knowledge of the infinite distance separating the splendor of the Father from our constitutional nothingness. For without humility, without the permanent notion of the divine Presence, heaven cannot reveal itself to us, Jesus cannot take us, and the Spirit cannot regenerate us.

Doubtless, all of this somewhat resembles a catechism lesson. But, to the most scientific theology, I prefer those simple, childish statements that so many educated Catholics consider as good only for the ignorant. In the world of intelligence also, extremes meet one another, and the only way to describe eternal realities with the least deformation is to express them in such a manner that they will enter into the heart of the meek, whom Jesus loves above all men.

⊕

Good comes from the Father, truth from the Son, beauty from the Spirit; faith comes from the Father, hope from the Son, charity from the Spirit. The Son, who is the perceptible form of the unknowable Being, is the command of the Father that plans the way. It is the Son (as the Word made flesh) who pronounces truth. It is the Spirit who manifests life.

These are the first impressions received by our intelligence when it tries to turn towards God. But how can we speak of the Spirit, since he passes through the most cohesive mental systems, since he escapes the efforts of the most sublime contemplatives? No one has thought or spoken of him save using gross images. Such hieratic symbols alone could subtilize us sufficiently to reach him, were he to condescend to hover over us. But who understands symbols but for the geniuses of art? Yet art is the most potent and efficacious beverage that spiritualizes our contemporaries.

To begin with, the awareness of beauty was primarily metaphysical. Later on, our pious ancestors gave it sentimental and psychological slants. The scientists of today recognize it only as sensation or instinct. Yes, all of this is very true, since man, built in the image of God, is essentially an organic unity wherein everything blends, corresponds, resounds, reacts reciprocally. He alone whose thoughts, sensitivity, and awareness vibrate in harmony, will recognize the symbols.

Attributing the sky-blue color to the Holy Spirit and the

The Trinity

greenish tones of the ocean waters to the Virgin teaches us nothing unless we feel the secret soul of the blue color and of the green color. Among the greatest painters are there but three who have ever guessed the ineffable language of colors? It does exist: the hermeneutic and liturgical traditions prove it. Thus, Jesus's robe is "blue" when he teaches and when he initiates, it is "red" when he heals and raises souls to heaven. In the first centuries, when the permanent relationship uniting the Virgin and the Holy Spirit had not been forgotten, one always clothed her in a blue robe. Among objects, the candid and intuitional Middle Ages attributed the flame to the Spirit; and among animals, they chose for him the dove, the sweetest of all winged creatures.

On the other hand, liturgy decrees that the priest wear a red chasuble for the Pentecost and other similar feasts. In fact, the Holy Spirit plays a dual role of circumincession.[1] First, being essentially active, positive, perturbing, he fecunds the primitive waters, ranges throughout the universe, penetrates all flesh in order to crucify, heal, and regenerate it. Or again, secondly, united mysteriously to the diaphanous substance of the celestial Virgin, he flows in the living waters, in the fountains of eternal life wherein the soul quenches itself, and where Christ washes us for the ultimate baptism.

We must take notice that all ecclesiastical traditions formally refuse to portray the Holy Spirit under human form. The reason being that when, from the inaccessible Father, the Spirit rushes towards the voluntarily exiled Son to the confines of creation, he is called Life. When, from the Son

---

[1] Circumincession: the reciprocal existence in each other of the three Persons of the Trinity. ED

(the voluntarily enchained slave in the darkest cells) the Spirit reascends with wings deployed towards the Father, he is called Love. When the same Spirit illumines, inflames, consoles, and brings harmony to opposites, he is called Beauty. And Life, Love, and Beauty are everywhere. The Spirit himself—multiform, mobile, ungraspable, essentially free—does not have to incarnate. Rather, he penetrates all flesh and all matter, from the most obscure to the more radiant, but never permits himself to be imprisoned by any, since he is the great liberator.

I dare tell what he also is: the perpetual executioner of Christ. Is it not love that impels Christ to slavery and martyrdom? Are not our crimes and selfishness, which torture Christ, born in the swamps and deserts where the vortex of the Spirit throws us? If we conquer, will it not be because Christ came to our rescue? If we succumb, will it not be again through Christ, still our savior? These are the extraordinary dramas where our liberty remains totally responsible, whether it goes to the light or towards the fire. These are catastrophes where love, thrown out of bounds by the violence of its state makes the gestures of hatred, then falls deeper into more ardent, profound, and serene love. Thus Jesus, who above is the master of the Spirit, makes himself here-below the slave of the Spirit; and so the gestures of the Father explode in lightning bursts upon the darkness of our primal ignorance.

But Jesus... slave... remains the master. Were he not there at the moment when the terrible courier of God precipitates himself upon the worlds and peoples, all would sink into the primitive abyss. The hatred of the enemies of Jesus serves providential designs; the infinity of the offense thus avoided, the infinity of the atonement disappears.

The Trinity

That is why the humble young girl to whom the angel reveals the great mystery is not troubled. Let us imitate her in the lesser surprises that daily life brings to us. Let us imitate her by always looking higher: the summits will communicate their sublime tranquility to us.

The Spirit passing over the marshes disturbs the fetid vapors and irritates their unclean inhabitants. He (splendor personified) chases shadows. He (beauty) makes the horrible seem more monstrous. He (love and fervor) excites anger or provokes indifference. He is the frightening cross upon whose infinite arms hangs the salvation of the world. He incites the sinful crowd onward, infusing them with intelligence, which they deform in view of martyrizing love. It is from him (truth itself) that lies, money, glory, power, and all other means by which we hide Christ from one another, draw their power. So that finally, humanity, having fallen to the extreme nadir, where death is all powerful, may rise again towards the ultimate zenith, where the same death dies for a multiplicity of unmeasured lives.

It is the Spirit who goads and perturbs and ravages our spirit until true prayer gushes out of it, until our fibers learn how to cry for mercy. The apostle Paul—the uncompromising Jew, the disciple of Gamaliel—knew very well which cavalier was whipping his people since Moses, when he wrote to the Romans (another inflexible race): "Christ saves us only for the future with hope."

Yes, it is true, Jesus brings us the greatest hope. But it is up to us to accept the Spirit whom Jesus left to us after his visit. The healer comes only for the sick, and his remedy is the Spirit. To our intelligence he prescribes truth. To our heart he restores purity. And to our body he gives health. We forsake anterior truth, purity, and beauty in order to find—

through errors, prostitutions, and diseases—ulterior truth, purity and beauty, which are also eternal, but unknown and inconceivable even to angels. Eternal life, which is the life of God, renews itself ceaselessly, while temporal existence can only transform itself. The "knots" of these transformations are called deaths. But, as an infinite multitude of eternal renewals are regulated with infinite speed, and as these innumerable births are organized according to perfect harmony, absolute motion appears to our philosophers as immobility, indifference, and immutability.

Hence the Spirit takes hold of us and makes us over, from top to bottom. He puts outside that which was inside. He raises the cells, those that bore our entire weight and the exertions of our walking, up to our brain. Thus is a mysterious virginity remade within a being. This new birth bears fruit only among very rare souls, among whom Mary holds first place. Primarily, she was judged worthy physically to become the mother of God because her spiritual virginity was perfect. A physical virtue is worthy only if, when born from within, it proceeds from moral virtue. Continence is worth nothing unless engendered by charity.

Let us then prostrate ourselves and admire this ineffable concert of miracles that only oppose one another in order to multiply, that only seem to fight in order to better fuse, and vanish only to be reborn again as more splendid and more adorable marvels. Let us look at Jesus, who exiles himself from the eternal palace, acting the part of a prodigal son. Let us look at the Spirit, who accompanies him as a translucid shadow, both as a faithful servant and as his pitiless driver. Let us imitate Jesus. Let us imitate his Mother—the rose that closes at the murmurings of this earth, the vase sealed against all the perfumes of here-below—a totally virginal being, who never received anything except through the most secretive angels.

You, too, put yourself in readiness for the divine visitation. Open your hearts only to the inspirations of love and to the favor of charity. Humility will give you its strength to bear all your tasks. And, like Mary performing her lowly tasks, when you will bend over ingrate faces, your hands, your eyes, and your words will pour upon them the regenerating Spirit who will transfigure them into precious masterpieces and into visages of light.

The Parents of Jesus

N THE SIXTH MONTH (after the annunciation of John) God sent the angel Gabriel to a city in Galilee, called Nazareth, to a virgin engaged to a man named Joseph of the house of David; and the virgin's name was Mary. The angel came unto her and said, Hail, thou who art full of grace, the Lord is with thee; blessed art thou among women. And when she saw the angel, she was perplexed at his saying and wondered in her mind what this salutation could be. So the angel said to her, Fear not, Mary, for thou hast found favor with God, and thou shalt conceive in thy womb and bring forth a son and thou shalt call his name: Jesus. He shall be great; he shall be called the Son of the Highest, and the Lord God shall give him the throne of his father David. He shall reign over the house of Jacob forever; and his kingdom shall have no end.

Then Mary said to the angel: How shall this be, seeing I know not a man? The angel answered, and said to her: The Holy Spirit shall come upon thee, and the power of the Highest will overshadow thee; therefore the child who will be born of thee and who will be holy shall be called the Son of God. Behold, thy cousin Elizabeth has also conceived a son in her old age; this is the sixth month with her who was called barren, for with God nothing shall be impossible. Mary said, Behold the handmaid of the Lord; be it unto me according to thy word. And the angel departed from her. (Luke 1:26–38)

While reading the admirable story of St Luke over again, let us enjoy the savor that exudes from it—imprecise at first, but so refreshing later. Do you not find that these thirteen verses, so touching and of such pure simplicity, even give evidence of man's worthlessness? They do not merely point it out. They imply, declare, and even affirm it. It becomes an accepted fact as an *a priori*. Initiative, will, important enterprises, and results painfully won—all add up to zero before God and before his angel.

This may seem harsh to you, men of the twentieth century, rightly proud of your efforts and your triumphs, circumvented as you are by the flattery of the Adversary's minions, inclined to heed their insidious advice on the cultivation of will, the acquisition of powers, and intellectual ambition. But take heed! Listen to the veritable voices from heaven. Fear not having to step down; you will rise all the better towards the holy mountain. Yet, do not forget that we must act, work, and toil even more than the most vigorous fighters of the prince of this world do.

⊕

Why did the incarnation of the Word take place in Galilee and in Judea? Why were Nazareth and Bethlehem chosen from among the hundreds of hamlets? Primarily because of the unfathomable divine will, but also for natural causes.

In fact, nothing happens anywhere without provoking repercussions. In the beginning, as soon as the Word appeared in this still very small universe, all the worlds that were to come out of these primitive worlds had to prepare for his visit. And the earth, among others, became oriented in space in such a way that the quality of the currents by means of which she communicates with the sun all during her life, would make her, at a stated epoch, ready for this visit. The invisible, on the other hand, is always localized in some point of the visible. Galilee and Bethlehem were the places where ended, at the instant of the incarnation, the direct line from the sun to the earth (from the dynamic center of the sun to the dynamic center of the earth)—in the manner of a lens which, when receiving the solar rays, sets wood afire only if it is placed exactly at its focus. Hence, the Word landed in the three kingdoms: in humanity, in the spirit of the earth, and at the exact places ready to receive him.

Judea was the country or region on earth of the creative principle. Galilee was the starting-point of the ontological cycles of our race: Nazareth was the chosen, sanctified, distinct spot. There she lived—the woman unique among all—this Virgin Mother, spoken of in all legends since the beginning of time.

Here is the hamlet nestling in the hills, the ascending streets, the cottage with a small garden, where a fig tree grows on the terrace. Through the open door, luminous light filtrates. Smell the odors of spring in the air, see the smiling hills, the diaphanic undulation of fields, the long olive groves, the paths cheerfully bordered with white flowering almond trees in bloom; here and there you will find a few cypress standing guard at a gate or a roadside.

Then one morning, just another among those perfumed days in this blessed countryside, as the Virgin is busily attending to her chores, she, herself still such a child, sees

The Parents of Jesus

the shadows of the little room deepen as if something at the door were curbing the solar rays: a visitor has suddenly entered. The same athlete with dreamy eyes who had already spoken to old Zacharias—the divine herald, the courier with tireless feet, the archangel Gabriel appears. His immaterial form overflows the confines of the little room. The glory emanating from him makes the brilliant sunlight appear livid. His floating robe, his wings, his translucid golden hair, melt into this sumptuous aura. The slender young woman who had receded into a corner seems like a long, blue shadow in the vibrating silver and iridescent luminosity that now fills the house.

The messenger bows before the slender form who contemplates him. And then, at long last, the wait of centuries is at an end. The sigh of generations is stilled. The salutation that will echo a thousandfold through the earth bursts forth: *Ave Maria*.

What solemn bearing had this sower with the flamboyant wings! If the voice of a puny phantom is sufficient to tear virile courage down, how strong must be the soul of this frail girl whose ears are being filled by the formidable voice of the messenger from the Almighty! Distant voice, strange voice, a voice wherein nothing human or earthly can be detected—echo of zodiacal solitudes, prolongation of tempests and fulgurations where worlds are being battered, a voice saturated with the majestic harmonies of the firmament. Too powerful a voice, whose weight would crush ordinary lungs, under whose vibrations the earth trembles, and our faces blanch to sepulchral pallor.

Can you visualize a being to whom God says: "Set this sun afire," and the sun burns! Or else: "Take away this race from Altair and transport it upon Arcturus," and half a billion men die! Imagine, if you can, the power of such an arm. See this giant who all of a sudden appeared through the walls that begin to crack. Listen to his calm, immutable voice still rumbling with the deafening thunder of echoes from the infinite! How agitated we would be!

But she, the very young girl, just out of the protective Temple, raises her eyes above her needlework and is merely perplexed. It is true that she will search to understand for a long time. But not to have been terrorized—is that not proof of the relative calm of her inner exaltation? Had not the soul of that child already lived in the society of angels!

Listen to the words of the Salutation, appreciate the savor of their veracity: Mary is "filled with grace."

The catechism's definition is short. "Grace" is a divine favor, the tenderness of the Father, that which he gives us without our meriting it. It also means the manner by which he gives us those admirable and mysterious gifts. We are hardly ever aware of the Father's overwhelming favors, still less do we feel the adorable kindness of his gestures. In the relationships he maintains with man, what we call "good" are his commandments; "truth" is the fruit of our obedience; "beauty" is the gratuity of our recompense that surpasses what we merit.

And the Virgin—who is the plenitude of these gifts—remains the goddess of true beauty, of the very beauty that is the luxury in the works of God, which brings ecstasy to the poet and the artist, that which finally shows us the humble woman of Bethlehem and the exiled woman of Egypt having become the queen of permanent riches and of perpetual glories. The force who stands before Mary brings her a triple torch—reflection of the divine Ternary. Reread the speech of the angel. "Full of grace"—is that not God's

The Parents of Jesus

own gift? The company of the Lord—is that not the Son himself? The peculiar benediction—is that not the Spirit's effluence?

We could all receive as much, were we willing. The mercy of the Father is a sun, but the eyes of the spectators remain closed. By contrast, a diamond in a dark room catches the faintest glimmer and transforms it into a lightning flash. The Virgin did just that with the ray of the Holy Spirit. Had her soul not desired the Savior with such intensity and consuming ardor, the shadow of the Almighty would not have descended and could not have descended upon her.

Mary does not understand how her child will be the Son of the Almighty—the sign, the witness, the living body of the infinite solicitude of the Father. But she accepts: "I am the servant of the Lord." Simple expression of the most sublime state of soul. May such simplicity give us back the taste for simplicity. Today, words are pompous and thoughts picayune. Would, on the contrary, that thoughts were grandiose! Expensive clothing does nothing for a measly body, but a noble form gives style to the cheapest clothing. Would that our words could be prosaic and our sentiments magnificent. For that, we must first of all be truthful. The man who sincerely means all he writes, who would not be lying as he writes at the bottom of a letter: "I remain, sir, your devoted servant"—that man would start growing in the sight of the Almighty that kind of growth beside which all earthly majesties are but servility.

Focus your eyes upon the state of the Virgin as servant of the Lord. We are all servants of someone, of ourselves most of the time, of our own passions and vices. The elite among humanity serve some of the regent gods of our natural ideals of wisdom and of beauty. Here and there a few rare ones serve the supernatural ideal: the Lord. How great, noble, and pure are those servants!

These remarks may seem insignificant. Nothing is insignificant. The passionate ardor that is the habitual state of soul of a disciple of Jesus needs an outer counterpart: practice. Our inner and outer life must be in concord, otherwise a disequilibrium occurs. Fear not to put the teachings of the gospel into practice. No matter how naive they seem, their source and their aim will make them useful and solemn. For instance, see in the scene of the Annunciation the perfect example of what our conduct should be. A constant effort towards fulfilling the duties of our daily life; then all of a sudden comes the extraordinary descent of an angel of the Lord. In spite of being perplexed, in spite of incomprehensibility, one must accept, and offer one's self to God immediately and totally. That is what made the Virgin so great. That is what our heart should be, if it really wants to receive Christ.

Admire the truth within evangelical scenes. If the left hand must be unknowing of the good done by the right hand, if true saintliness is the one that ignores itself, all the more so should a repentant and burning soul not be aware that it has reached the desolate depths of repentance, or when it ascends to the extreme incandescence of love. That is why the sudden apparition of the angel surprises the Virgin. That is why she welcomes, although without very well understanding, the annunciation of the divine descent—the unique object of her sighs and tears: "At midnight the Bridegroom appears…"

⊕

Let us leave the physical scene of the Annunciation aside in order to scrutinize its background: from it, we will draw out the same maxims. Let us enter, I pray you, into this very unknown universe God has built to maintain contact with us. Here, the Father is one pole; we are the other (a nothing, a mathematical abstraction). Between him and us the immense stature of the Savior stands, and the infinite processions of the Paraclete are deployed.

This is the universe triple and one: of grace, of the presence, and of benediction. Mary was its first inhabitant; she became its guiding genius.

St Thomas defines God as pure act. The least of his movements creates. When he gives us something, this grace is a spark of the Word, therefore a presence; this gift is a regenerating force, therefore a benediction. You see Mary filled with supernatural favors—consequently God is really there at her side; she is endowed with the Spirit. Everything is related in the kingdom of harmony; and its revelators separate the various phases of its manifestations only to make it more intelligible to us.

We already know that before nature, before other men, and face to face with the gods, man may be somebody and sometimes a master—but before God, in the universe of grace—he is nothing. Needless for us to follow the minute analyses that theology makes of the different modes of grace; they are not necessary to us. Facing the justice of God, it is sufficient for us to have accepted the nothingness of our efforts and of our merits. His love will then extend its powerful and merciful hand, pouring his treasures upon us, as if there had been merit in what we had done. Mary silently teaches us that we must perceive that the very energy we expend in fighting desperately for existence is but a gratuitous grace.

When we attain that state of soul, God comes with us.

Christ accompanies us. Jesus supports our faltering steps. Imagine the master of the earth bending over the first swelling of a bud with solicitude. Were that bud to feel his concern, what gratitude it would exude!

How filled with beatitude are the days of a disciple, even in the midst of great pain! He walks in the shadow of his Friend; he is clothed with the mantle of faith; his spirit hears eternal words; a powerful arm sustains him; at intervals, Jesus takes hold of him and lifts him above the surrounding crowd. What are the marvels that fill the eyes of the disciple in ecstasy? They are the ineffable presence of the One whom his heart seeks and has always loved; fatal and revivifying delights, transports, agonies, flights; sacred dramas whose actors pass in front of his eyes sometimes, hidden beneath the mantle of humility—Mary has experienced all of these, and through her they come back to transfigure those among men who have become purified.

What does it mean "to bless"? It is wishing good; it is using the faculty possessed by our wishes that makes them come true. Our ancestors were aware of that force, and the Anglo-American psychists of today are merely repeating an old story. But our thought is never completely pure, nor ever completely effective. The blessing, alone, that comes from heaven becomes effective *in toto*—because it is the projection of the kindness of the Father—it alone, among billions, brings fruit even to the physical world. "The Father alone is Good."

Our eyes are not sensitive to goodness. The spiritual universe is composed of several aspects: the aspect of grandeur, of complexity, of blood, selfishness, terror, beauty. One may find numerous men who can detect, more or less clearly, these various faces of life. Rarer are those to whom

The Parents of Jesus

the true face of benevolence is revealed, because very rare are those who by means of their every physical action direct their spirit towards veritable goodness. Those who carry divine lights within themselves all affirm that the universe is an immense benediction.

To penetrate deeper into the profound meaning of this saying, one must recognize Jesus as the perfect model of benediction. Thus the angel characterizes him through his double lineage, both as Son of the Most High and as son of David, because any benediction is the answer to an expressed or tacit demand, and the benedictions that come from God are eternal.

The birth of Jesus Christ came about this way: when his mother Mary was engaged to Joseph, before they came together, she was found with child of the Holy Spirit. Then Joseph, her husband, being a just man and not willing to make her a public scandal, wanted to leave her secretly. But as he thought on these things, the angel of the Lord appeared to him in a dream, saying: Joseph, son of David, fear not to take Mary as thy wife; for that which she has conceived is of the Holy Spirit. She shall bring forth a son and thou shalt call his name Jesus, for he shall save his people from their sins. Now all this was done so that which the Lord spoke by the prophet might be fulfilled: Behold, a virgin shall conceive, shall bring forth a son and they shall call him Emmanuel, which means: God with us. Then Joseph awakened from his sleep, did as the angel of the Lord had bidden him, and took unto him his wife. But he knew her not till she had brought forth her first-born son, and he called his name Jesus. (Matthew 1:18–25)

This is one of the most human and touching figures of the New Testament. The humble spouse of the Virgin lived a mediocre existence, like the immense majority of men. The personages of the bible, whenever separated from the prestige of liturgies and apologetics, are simple people. It is good to see them such as they lived: it shows us the soil of the deep valleys in which God places the seeds of his masterpieces; it encourages us all, since we are all unhappy with our fate.

The personage and name of Joseph can give birth to many intellectual teachings in the spirit of the contemplative. Tradition states that he was a carpenter, and by this means the whole system of symbolic Freemasonry is clarified. Freemasonry, no matter what certain contemporary polemicists say—that is, the veritable masonry—was Christian till the thirteenth century. Then its spirit altered, it is true. But its forms remained Christian. And it will be to the glory of Cagliostro for having dedicated his life in attempting to purify this vast body in turmoil.[1]

Joseph[2] was the protector of the mystery of the Incarnation. This, Thomas Aquinas and Bossuet, with their good common sense, clearly saw. Here is the explanation: the

---

[1] Each Masonic system (degree) represents or recalls an initiation. The Scottish Rite is the most normal: in the first degrees, it gives a moral preparation; from the 4th to the 17th degrees, the traditional notions of Hermeticism are developed, as well as the unfolding of its principles in history. The 18th degree, that of the Rose-Croix, is essentially Christian: it praises the essential act of all religion as having received its ultimate

The Parents of Jesus

Father organized the world like an enclosed field where two equal forces battle: his, or rather the portion of his all-powerfulness necessary to universal life, and the power of the Adversary, equal and opposed, to the former. Please note that this other power comes from the same Creator. When the Father, who is all-goodness, wanted to save this world by his Son, the Adversary could have retarded that salvation; everything had to be kept in secret till the physical body of Jesus was strong enough for resistance. On the other hand, it was essential that the Word, in his Incarnation, follow the common path. The work would have been truncated if the Word had suddenly risen in the stature of a man, or if he had been content to choose a medium for himself—as in an avatar—and to concentrate upon him his influence and power. On the other hand, the Adversary keeps well informed of all that happens in the world. He has his own means of inspection. His police—the most vigilant there is—watches what men think and how they feel.

The oncoming birth of the Word in that particular family and in that particular city had to be concealed; for that, even the spouses themselves, though informed of the im-

---

form from Christ. From the 19th to the 30th degree are delineated the works of the adept in the Temple and among people; occult sciences, ecstasies, social adaptations. The final three degrees represent the adept out of the Temple fulfilling among a people the mission for which he was predestined. But let us note that this is but the outer interpretation of the teachings of the gospel: it is their reflection in the world of the will. Should we call attention to the fact that Cagliostro's first name was Joseph?

[2] In kabbalistic language, this name represents the etheric space between the earth and the moon and its currents; or the manifestation of light, until then captive, in the folds of the serpent. Cf. *L'Annonciateur*, by Villiers de l'Isle-Adam: "Helcias disappeared in a fulguration."

portance of their mission, must not really know exactly of what it consisted, because even had their mouths remained mute, their hearts would have permitted admiration and transports to gush forth; and the henchmen of hell thus would have discovered the way of the miracle.

Joseph played an indispensable role. If Judea had known the secret of the birth of Jesus, everyone would have been scandalized. Just as, if it were proven to us that the good we do does not come from us, our pride, too violently crushed, would not leave us sufficient strength to carry on. So that Christ could seemingly follow the usual law, Joseph was placed there in order to prevent scandal, and to furnish for the witnesses (those still incapable of believing) an excuse for their blind obstinacy. Let us have the courage—yes, us—to look at our nothingness face to face, and to face the truth about ourselves. The apparent paternity of Joseph gives us the key to true regeneration. Man never reaches heaven—the veritable heaven of the Father—by his own forces, or by the help of a master, living or dead, or by the assistance of any god. Heaven alone leads us towards itself. It is heaven that gives everything, even to the repentance that seems to be born from our very depths or from an exterior religious influence. It is through the angels of heaven that the seed of conversion is able to sprout within us: but to do this they hide, because of internal and external enemies, just as they kept hidden once upon a time in order for divine mercy to be realized in the person of the child Jesus.[3] In short, at the descent of the Word, it was necessary that all doors be closed, but one.

---

[3] And yet heaven, which gives us everything, only grants its gifts when our efforts towards it have reached the ultimate limits of their

The Parents of Jesus

And when, later, Christ will recommend to us not to hide the light, he will on the other hand warn us not to throw holy things to dogs. If he orders us to be as simple as doves, he immediately adds: and wise as serpents. Thus, to better understand him, it is necessary for us to experience, successively, the greatest possible number of opposing viewpoints.

⊕

Let us look, if you please, at the foster-father of Christ in order to derive some lessons from his example. Joseph is the man of silence, the man of the night, the man of mystery, the man of dreams. His whole existence is governed by four dreams: he heeds them and fulfills them by four acts of the rarest sort of obedience. Collaborator of the Father and informed of providential plans—he keeps silent. He is the safest of confidants—he who could reveal so many startling things. Millions of men speak without motive, ceaselessly, fruitlessly. Just as his bride, he too is the keeper of several secrets. One may, when contemplating attentively, see in the intimate being of this workman the model of an initiator of the highest category. Because his domain is silence, and his teaching is given without uttering a word.

The crowds need noise; but silence is essential to those who, in the depths, hear the angels fly, the celestial harmo-

---

strength. You may call these paradoxes or insoluble antinomies. No. This situation regarding our liberty towards grace is understandable when one realizes that it bridges two modes or two worlds. It is the tangence of the human with the divine. And in order to understand it, any theoretician must neither place himself in one or the other of these planes, but, through an extraordinary feat of equilibrium, be astride both at the same time.

nies unfold—and those rising, ineffable songs next to which our most genial music is but discordant noise. How many things there are, far beyond us: one does not speak during stress. Those whose spirit works ceaselessly, like to keep quiet. Silence is the brother of solitude and of night, two beloved goddesses of the great workers and givers of comfort and calm.

Joseph, the silent one, receives from the evangelist the most magnificent praise: "He was a just man." That is all.[4] To be "just" means attaining equilibrium; it is maintaining equal balance among all the adverse tendencies whose battlefield is man. That implies a constant exercising of force as well as a perfect knowledge of things. Joseph, the vigorous workman, is too busy working to take time out for discourses. So, the Church has, by a significant antiphrase, consecrated to this "mute" Wednesday, the day priorly ruled by the god of eloquence. Mercury (that is, Hermes, whom the Greeks borrowed from the Egyptians) or the Masonic Hiram, still directed the souls and spirits beyond the dark gates. Mythologies, though profoundly differing in their basic principles, show us gods fulfilling analogous offices. And it is because the spirit of Joseph has accomplished the work of a teacher and of an initiator in the spiritual worlds, that his feast day has been assigned to March 19.[5] Nineteen is the number of the Holy City, of the carpenter's hatchet. March 19 is a day of the last week ruled by the sign Pisces, which is a dual sign, like all invisible beings whose hierophants once announced revelations. The Fishes

---

[4] It is believed, according to St Epiphanius and the Eastern Church, that St Joseph died a widower at the age of 81.

[5] Cf. the Brahmanic *Dakshinamurti.*

The Parents of Jesus

have always been the mute and living hieroglyphics of individual life, of apostolic aims, and of the Savior himself.

Catholicism contains singular truths. Generally speaking, in the line of knowledge, it realizes this statement of Simeon that Christ "overthrows the mighty and exalts the meek," because, if Catholicism retains the ontological functions just as the ancient sages had discovered them, it displaces and inverts them, giving new positions to their titularies.

Thus, in Joseph, the Church glorifies the humble father of a family, and the workman—the least mysterious and least cultured of all types. But in the esoteric kingdom of which this world is but a shadow, she attributes to Joseph the most secret vigilance. She regards this soul as the initiatrix par excellence since she names Joseph "light of patriarchs." She assimilates that soul to the ancient Raphael, to the master of vital currents, to the healer, to Asclepius, to the Açwins (healer gods of the Brahmins), since she indicates him as the hope of the sick. She brings him close to the Memphite Hermanubis, to the Yama of Benares, since she invokes him as patron of a holy death. Finally, extolling St Joseph as conqueror of demons, she renews word-for-word the praises addressed in the ancient temples to all the Januses, the Jasons, the Thoths, the Rishis, by whose interventions the poor humans resist infernal attacks.

May these interconnections, as cursory as they are, make us aware of the wealth of unexplored treasures that the letter of our religion keeps hidden. But, let us not become hypnotized over them either: they are the outer marvel, but there are many other virtues and other magnificences in the gospel, and it is towards those only that I wish to lead you. They are inexpressible. I cannot describe them to you. But, "Come and see."

THE CHILDHOOD OF JESUS

⊕

Let us, in all simplicity, look at the text. Here is an elderly man in whose heart the profound dawn of love is rising. He loves a young girl with that nuance of depth warranted by the difference in their ages. In his eye, she is all pure, lily-like, candid, marvelous, unique. Then, all of a sudden, something apparently attacks this celestial flower. What a disaster! His heart is lacerated. But his only thought is to safeguard the honor of the one who, to all semblance, might be unworthy. He tries to find her an honorable retreat.[6] It is then that the angel intervenes and asks of him an additional effort.

The intervention comes in a dream. I will not repeat the apology for, or the theory of dreams. You will know, as I often have stated, that the dream is the surest, most normal, and certain method of getting in touch with the invisible. In sleep, we generally see more or less symbolic pictures. But Joseph, like the patriarchs (and as we too will do when we will have become "just"), sees a being or an angel. For our dreams to be true, exact, clear, there is but one sufficient and necessary condition: that we live body, soul, and mind in truth. At least, that we attempt living as "the just."

Who is the angel Gabriel? There are two currents in cosmic life: one ascends, the other answers by descending from heaven to help it. The angel is one of the waves of the latter. Organic laws, spiritual centers, innate properties, mental modes, psychic states, and sciences are some of those waves.

Angels construct our moral state. They are individual and

---

[6] Cf. Psalms 91:1: "Whoever dwells in the shelter of the Most High will rest in the shadow of the Almighty." That is, he who is anchored in the first world is beyond the attacks of destiny.

The Parents of Jesus

immaterial beings. They are grouped by functions around one of their own who has received a stronger will. They bring, so to speak, into existence our thoughts, feelings, and acts that, were it not for their call, would often remain buried in the deep layers of our being. Little by little, an angel builds himself a body or a representation of himself on earth: a family, an association, a profession, a botanical, zoological, and human species are all angelic bodies. A man who, like St Vincent de Paul or Bach, is totally absorbed in one function, is an angel, either good or bad.

In this particular case at hand, the terrestrial parents of Jesus had to live from then on under the absolute power of only one sentiment: one of mystery, silence, and incomprehensibility. They had to be the guardians of the child, materially and immaterially. A certain state of soul had to be created and developed within them, till it had usurped their entire personality until death. That is the work of the angel.

As for us, who obstinately hope to become in our soul nature what Joseph and Mary were so admirably in the physical, let us carefully heed our dreams. Awaited prayerfully, registered with exactitude, studied with calm common sense, they can be of invaluable help to us. By this means, our eyes and ears will open—just as Christ recommended to his disciples.

⊕

Another point to be considered are the two names of the Messiah which the angel and the prophet indicated: Jesus and Emmanuel.

Among the wisdoms of humankind, none admit the Messiah to be the Son of God; but a few teachings, such as Bahaism, believe him to be the son of a virgin. The knowledge of the spiritual identity of Jesus belongs to the supra-intellectual order, and is consequently indemonstrable[7]; it is a gift analogous to the esthetic or moral sense. It is possible, however, to reach that understanding by striving to feel what the two names, Jesus and Emmanuel, represent.

There is a virtue in names: a virtue other than that of hieroglyphics; a more fragrant perfume than the one they emit when compressed within folios. It is needless to enter into the esoteric considerations of the Hebraic tetragram and Shin so as to know how the name of Jesus can be dissected (Johann Reuchlin and Louis-Claude de Saint-Martin have fully done so); neither should we bother to explain why the vowel dots change Joshua into Jesus, or what associations link Emmanuel with the Manu, the Minos, or the Numa of polytheism.

Better to keep our hearts as fresh and calm as the beauty of the countryside in the spring. Let us push aside our fears, worries, feelings of remorse, and problems. Let us become like joyous children who play in the light. Then we may be able to feel the approaching glories of that all-powerful name. Maybe those two divine syllables will reveal to us the Creator of beings, the strength of the Father, the perfect image of heaven, the manifestation of eternity, this constantly active, untiring will that satisfies everywhere, anywhere, at all times, the mystical aspiration of creatures. We

---

[7] The methods, used by the Kabbalah give some relative proofs concerning this truth; here is one: In Greek, the name of Jesus (Iesous) = 888; in Hebrew, the word Messiah = 345. The aphorism: The Being is the Being (Ayeh Asher Ayeh) = 543 (the preceding number being read from right to left). So, 345 + 543 = 888. On the other hand, the numbers of Joseph: 156; Mary: 248; and Truth: 484—when added, also give 888. Such demonstrations, however, are nothing but games for the spirit.

will be able to perceive the dazzling form of the One who is the Friend, the Savior, and the Bridegroom. We will know why the name of Jesus, when pronounced with all of our forces united, makes the angels, the demons, and the elements prostrate themselves. Finally, we will understand how Christ alone is the only one worthy to be called Emmanuel: "God with us."

In fact, he is with us, not just from the height of his celestial throne or through the powerful outpourings of his divine compassion, or by the ministry of his servants whom he sends us, or through the influence of his spirit. He was among us physically two thousand years ago; he visited a great many more countries than is believed; and many other peoples besides the Israelites were able to see his august face and to sustain the divine delights of his gaze. I declare and repeat to you who believe, in truth, that Christ Jesus is the only Son of God—that you know this only because you met him once upon a time either in some city of the Empire, in the Celtic forests, in the Libyan deserts, in the jungles or mountains, or upon vast, uncharted seas.

To anyone but him, to assume the title of Emmanuel would suffice, but these labors do not sate the love that consumes him. Not only did he come on earth: he has *remained* here. Several men, who gave themselves body and soul to his service, have received his visit (his visits, I should rather say); for a few, even, the real divine Presence has remained constantly at hand. In each of us, the "Emmanuel" has left a parcel of himself. All of us, even the most vile, carry within ourselves, above and beyond the living light given to us at creation, a seed of the Word. Let us nurture it, and we will become friends of Christ. Let us remember those things. Let us recall them to our body, heart, and thoughts ceaselessly.

Let us attempt every moment of the day to become new Emmanuels for each creature that God has placed beside us; enthusiastic and scrupulous copyists of the One who has given us such encouragement:

"To do the will of my Father who is in heaven, is to be my brother, to be my father, to be my mother." Through this revealed promise, may the infinite horizons exalt us beyond ourselves forever!

The Magnificat

ARY AROSE in those days and went into the hill country with haste into a city of Judea. She entered into the house of Zacharias and saluted Elizabeth. It came to pass that when Elizabeth heard the salutation of Mary, the babe leaped in her womb; and Elizabeth was filled with the Holy Spirit. She spoke out with a loud voice, and said, Blessed art thou among women, and blessed is the fruit of thy womb. And why is it that the mother of my Lord should come to me: For, lo, as soon as the voice of the salutation sounded in my ears, the babe leaped in my womb for joy. Blessed is she who believed in the fulfillment of those things that were told her from the Lord. And Mary said, My soul doth magnify the Lord, and my spirit rejoices in God my Savior, for he has regarded the low estate of his handmaiden; for, behold, from henceforth all generations shall call me blessed. For the Almighty has done to me great things; and holy is his name. And his mercy is on them that fear him from generation to generation. He has shown strength with his arm; he has dissipated the designs that the proud formed in their heart. He has put down the mighty from their seats, and exalted them of low degree. He has filled the hungry with good things, and has sent away the rich empty-handed; he helped his

servant Israel, in remembrance of his mercy; as he had spoken of it to our fathers, to Abraham and to his posterity forever. And Mary abode with her about three months, then returned to her own house. (Luke 1:39–56)

Right after the visit of the angel, Mary arises in haste and leaves to rejoin her elderly cousin. Joseph accompanies her, walking by the side of the lowly little donkey whose hoofs stay steady among the stones of the mountain trails. These travelers are really poor folk. The man carries a little money in his belt; the pack-saddle bears some foodstuffs and a modest gift for their relatives. How charming must that trip have been as they crossed brooks and hills, orchards and olive groves; as they ascended slowly through terraces under cultivation, rested at midday in the copsewood of shady ravines, and enjoyed the august evenings descending with their grand and noble peace—and the stars and lunar nights in the spring!

They are now approaching the old, rough-hewn stone house of Zacharias, such as one finds in the Provençe today. Hastening to greet them from the arcade at the top of the outside stairway, the elderly couple appear. Do you hear the effusions, the simplicity of this welcome? Notice their attentive care—the hot water to bathe the dusty feet of the travelers, the frugal supper, the donkey being provided for in the darkened stable that is hewn out of the rock itself. Listen to the slow, measured conversations, the startled expressions, the low exclamations; listen to the ritual prayer of the two men under the moon, which is at her zenith, while the two women are still exchanging confidences. What an admirable sight, where inner beauty corresponds exactly to the beauty of the decor! But, were our personages

The Magnificat

to return today, their joys would be less serene and their concern more worrisome in our modern life, from which nobility has fled!

One wonders for what reason the visit of the Virgin to her cousin is recounted. It was a simple errand; what lesson does it convey? Socially, Mary is one step below Elizabeth; spiritually, she is far beyond her. From the heavenly standpoint, there are two valid reasons for recounting this trip: divine Law demands that we observe customs and habits; and it also advocates that the superior owes something to the lesser. Mary satisfies both observances.

Before God, all hierarchic positions have equal functions. It is only to us that they seem to be high or low: this classification is merely relative. In order to prevent an anarchistic error on one hand and an absolutist error on the other, one must weigh the two points of view. Thus, the frank collaboration between the leaders and the led can occur without any underlying designs from either.

Mary thus fulfills social proprieties as follows. There are two kinds of politeness. One, such as ours, is merely that of decorum: it satisfies courteous formulae without the heart vivifying them; it is a lie; it engenders the fruits of lies: slanders, envy, and discords. As regards the other: in true politeness, flowers bloom from the fertile ground of benevolence, compassion, and modesty. Politeness flows spontaneously from the state of soul wherein each of us considers himself to be the servant of others, ready to help and to encourage them; and because of its charm, our prosaic life finds itself bathed in smiling enchantment. Politeness is the luxury of our social contacts. Man not only needs material comfort, but he also has need for beauty. Mere necessities are sufficient, yet a little of the superfluous is indispensable for him.

Some people wear shabby clothes, yet think as "grand masters." Life in straitened circumstances can become sumptuous because of the wealth and beauty of their sentiments. Man can only be crushed materially. In his inner life, all wealth, magnificence, majesties, and powers are his. This is not mere phraseology, since all has influence upon all, since the most subtle force always ends by operating transformations within matter. Even an artist who has never left his studio, or a philosopher whose speculations have never been published, or even a hermit isolated in the desert—provided they have consumed themselves in their search for their ideal—force it to descend. They acclimatize it slowly to the heavier atmospheres of our earth; and imperceptibly its general state of mind, social levels, and opinions are being modified by the hidden influence of the forgotten efforts of some anonymous workman.

After two or three (never more than seven) generations pass without its happening—public intelligence finds itself enriched with new ideas; or else some legislator promulgates some humanitarian laws; or an inventor discovers a way to better material conditions.

One does not realize that the most positive activities spring from secret roots within the human heart. Take industrial life, for instance. If one could trace back into the beyond as far as to the living organic prototype whose materialization has furnished the locomotive, the automobile, or the airplane, one would be surprised to find the sacrifice of some previously unsung hero.

This should make us doubly aware of the importance of each act in our daily life. We do not know when a smile, a glance, or a kind gesture may engender transformations!

The Magnificat

⊕

Let us return to the Visitation. Elizabeth was to be the mother of the "greatest among men." Look at all the admirable women in history who became mothers of great men; how they built the character and sensitivity of these exceptional children through strife and labors. And, as the Baptist was the greatest among men, how rich and endowed his mother had to be in order to be able to weave for this extraordinary soul a terrestrial envelope capable of withstanding and keeping its flame alive.

That is why the Visitation was necessary.

Each being radiates upon all other beings. Do we not feel better or worse according to the spiritual level of those around us? Have we not at some time received from a passer-by some good, or experienced evil? The beings who are powerful either in good or in evil need not speak or act to exercise their supremacy. They appear, and that suffices—because the spirit of man radiates his own prestige automatically. It is up to us to analyze these impressions in order to welcome them, or banish them. Thus, the spirit of the Precursor, still in the limbo of gestation, recognizes the spirit of his master hidden under similar opaque veils, and he stirs—such is the virtue of spiritual contacts. Let us realize, so that our hopes will remain exalted, that the power of such radiation is more victorious when it springs from the very source of Verity. To the eyes of the seer, at that moment there occurred in the world of invisible realities the poignant meeting between the oldest among all "soldiers" and the greatest of all rulers.

The birth of a soul upon earth is a resultant. For instance, if a child is to be born ten years from now in this very room, if we had clear vision, we should already be able to discern the work of the double, and the first labors of the spirit who is endeavoring to throw anchor upon terrestrial depths in the ocean of existence. We treat these dynamic movements, whose frequency make them appear insignificant to us, rather lightly. We should give them our profoundest attention. As intermediaries between the visible and the invisible worlds, our functions are weighty. Let us accomplish them with goodwill and be constantly concerned with not falling short of the task.

In this scene of the Visitation, the three actors, Mary, Elizabeth, and Zacharias, are visibly transported above and beyond themselves. A supernatural hand activates them. They seem to us as a field being ravaged by a cyclone, and yet which remains unwitting of the dramas being played upon its stage. In such circumstances, the human being is said to be in a dream state. He pronounces words without understanding them; the Spirit possesses him; the meaning of things escapes him; and other men sometimes have to wait for centuries to learn of the mysteries that had been discussed then. Why is this? Because mysteries are alive: mysteries are angels. They express themselves in a superhuman language, though their interpreters employ human words.

"Blessed is she who believed those things which were told her from the Lord," said Elizabeth. This is the second circumstance where, in the gospel account, appears the idea of faith. To believe is a supra-intellectual act. To understand something is to incarnate it within our mental state. To believe in something means to act conformably with a light not yet perceptible, that the tautest stretch of our spirit barely permits us to guess the existence thereof. That is how, in the midst of the blackest shadows on stormy

The Magnificat

nights, the eye of the watcher already sees less darkness—there, where the dawn will rise only a few hours later.

The act of believing demands a precise filiation between our heart and a certain mystery. To believe in something false means that error still dwells in our very center. To believe in incomprehensible, and even inconceivable, truth demands moral purity, and to be overshadowed by that truth. And as "birds of a feather flock together," so do the just and the humble attract truth, while evil or vain men attract error.

That is why Mary gives this answer to Elizabeth: "My soul doth magnify the Lord."

The ten verses of this response, reminiscently constructed like the Psalms and Prophecies, are designated as a canticle or hymn. What is a hymn?

First, let us examine the universe under the two aspects of truth and beauty. Because creation lies in error, we wrongly attribute materialism to the concept of truth, because the majority of men hold as true or real only that which is material. For them, beauty is unreal—it is merely poetry or literature. For them, in serious life one speaks in prose; and it is only for entertainment, on the stage, that one sings and speaks in verse.

And yet, any truth necessarily contains some beauty. Truth and goodness that do not possess a little of the superfluous luxury of beauty are neither completely true nor good. Man, when in a lowly state, converses only with the residue of the movements of life, only with that which is decomposed in life. But, if he is afire, if a torch illumines him, if pain or joy transport him, the necessity of adopting an extraordinary mode of expression compels him to sing. Only those who carry magnificence within themselves sing: otherwise they are nothing but more or less clever actors.

When we are oppressed by some superhuman presence, a new kind of language becomes necessary. And so, art is the admirable effort of our powerlessness sublimated, which is then transmuted into power. It is the vigor of our stammering lips whose inebriation is finally tamed by a living will—that is why we should make friends among artists and poets; they will help us fill our anemic, prosaic surroundings with the ineffable.

The canticle or hymn of the Virgin explains with simplicity the eternal essence of beauty. She says: "My soul doth magnify the Lord"; and: "My spirit has rejoiced in God my Savior."

Now, the soul is our principle of eternity: autonomous, immutable, all serene; the inspiration and witness to every part of ourselves. It is the indestructible canal through which flows the water of the eternal fountain; it is the fixed center around which turn all bodies and planets, the sum-total of which constitutes our spirit. Its life is love, an endless canticle of beatitude, praise, and thankfulness.

The spirit, in whose enclosure character, personality, temperament, constitution, thought, soulfulness, and self gravitate as do the stars in the zodiac—that spirit is the sum-total of what nature has loaned the soul to work through. Consequently, the spirit labors, merits, and demerits. Invincibly, it leans towards eternal light. It only attains its normal stasis when it becomes grafted upon God, upon the Savior, our Jesus—the only form of God accessible to us. Then, embracing its ideal, its Bridegroom, "the spirit rejoices" in the ecstasy of mystical betrothal.

The Magnificat

The soul knows the aims of the different organisms that clothe her, which is why she alone can "magnify" the Lord. But man, the spirit of man, does not know the soul: his aim is, precisely, to attain this living cognizance. That which the Church calls mysteries are phenomena belonging to the world of the soul. They may be interpreted according to the physical, philosophical, scientific, sociological, or moral viewpoints. Thus are systems born. They are merely images: one cannot understand their very essence unless one has first received the baptism of the Spirit.

The soul does not need to be saved, since it does not fall. But the rest of the human being is perpetually exposed to the crystallizing forces of individualism and of nothingness. This is the Savior's very reason for being.

Let us not drop this idea before having seen how this first stanza of the *Magnificat* exposes the essential theory of beauty.

The soul corresponds to the always inaccessible ideal, if one limits the meaning of the word "always" to the finite duration of time.

The spirit corresponds to the man who scales the rugged paths of the mystical mountain, over the top of which hovers the ideal.

The ideal is the sum-total of all that which we know exists, but which we cannot yet see, understand, or possess—it is beauty; it is the plenitude of our aspirations; it is God. The spirit is ourselves; it is that which aspires and expires; it is desire and all desires; it is will; it is the hunger and thirst for happiness that kills us one and all. Let us carefully choose the mode for our happiness; the mode under which we feel God.

THE CHILDHOOD OF JESUS

⊕

The Virgin humbles herself; she understands the laws of spiritual dynamics; she knows that creatures alienate themselves from God by vaunting themselves—because created heights are akin to nothingness, while the uncreated reunites in the central depths of the world. Her spirit reached this admirable attitude as follows.

When man is sent to the universe, he believes he can walk alone; he believes only in himself; he does not want to be helped. Just like any reckless child, he falters and gets hurt. This is pride. However, after falling many times, he begins to notice his weakness and inexperience; he learns how to ask for help. All of us, no matter how many times we have reincarnated, still appear as mere little children under the light of truth.

The love with which the Father surrounds us, plus his grace, gives us strength and guides us through safer roads. The better we know ourselves, the more we are aware of our weakness. Whoever pretends being able to walk alone errs and is responsible for his tardiness and for the fate of his followers, visible or invisible. Whoever refers himself to heaven, once his duties are accomplished, frees himself from the shackles of destiny; divine aid remains his, permanent and constant.

The verses of the *Magnificat* relating to the proud, the powerful, and rich, may be explained in three ways.

Socially, if someone occupies a larger place and takes more power and fortune than his share should be, if he employs illegal means, cheats his fellow citizens—he causes an inevitable reaction and provokes disorder.

From the cosmic standpoint, man also tries to dominate by using forbidden means: summons, forced collaboration,

The Magnificat

and pacts with the invisible. In this manner, he forces beings to go out of their normal channel. Therefore, the physical plane receives forces that, though not necessarily evil, are not always adapted to it. This results in disorganizations here, below, above, and beyond.[1]

Finally, pride, tyranny, and the thirst for wealth are tendencies within us that—by reaction—must eventually produce humility, charity, and a desire for the divine. We think we owe our commercial or political success to our capabilities, energies, or powers of adaptation; but these means are effects, not causes. In the soul, in the universe, or in society, the advent of the Word recasts each being there where he belongs, he forces ill-gotten gains to be returned and reestablishes justice.

That is why, throughout its development, Christianity has brought about individual conversions, social upheavals, and cosmic upheavals. All of these alterations have occurred throughout all imaginable worlds. Therefore, the title of Restorer given to Christ has been entirely justified, as well as the active, special, and personal protection that the Father extends to any man dedicated to his service. Heaven never takes back what it has given; it gives perpetually, and the hitherto faithful servant who temporarily betrays his

---

[1] This would be the time to describe the upheaval which the Word's descent caused in the cosmic currents by forcing them back to the boundaries of creation. One would see that, in fact, the etheric waters battering against his rigid way changed the direction of their flux (flow), displacing hierarchies, and rolling to the left and downward that which flowed to the right and upward. Among other consequences, one would see here the ruin of the occult and divining sciences of antiquity. But to describe this would mean going beyond our plan and the limits of this essay.

master for a week, or for centuries, neither provokes the anger nor the vengeance of God: his inconstancy only erects a wall between the kindness of God and himself. That is how we must understand the love bestowed upon us.

The Canticle of Zacharias

HEN HIS FATHER, Zacharias, was filled with the Holy Spirit, and prophesied, saying, Blessed be the Lord God of Israel for he has visited and redeemed his people; and has raised up a horn of salvation for us in the house of his servant David; as he had spoken through the mouth of his holy prophets which have been since the world began: that we should be saved from our enemies, and from the hand of all that hate us; to perform the mercy promised to our fathers and to remember his holy covenant according to the oath which he swore to our father Abraham, that he would grant unto us, that after being delivered out of the hand of our enemies, we might serve him without fear, in holiness and righteousness before him, all the days of our life. And thou, child, shalt be called the prophet of the highest, for thou shalt go before the face of the Lord to prepare his ways; to give knowledge of salvation unto his people by the remission of their sins through the tender mercy of our God who from on high has looked upon us; and the rising sun will appear to give light to them that sit in darkness and in the shadow of death; to guide our feet into the ways of peace. The child grew, and waxed strong in spirit, and was in the deserts till the day he manifested in Israel. (Luke 1:67–80)

Zacharias prophesied. What is prophecy? The prophet stands above the diviner. To divine or foretell is a science and an art discovered by man. It means synthesizing correspondences, collecting conjectures, calling forth probabilities, diagnosing the future from the present—just as a doctor who, from external signs, follows the symptom back to its functional cause. Divination resembles positive science. Theoretically, it is true; in practice, merely venturesome. The future may be found within a horoscope or within the intricate lines of the palm. But the combination of all these elements may mount up to thousands. Patience cannot exhaust them, nor extract from them a mathematically exact conclusion. The diviner fills the voids with his intuition: his science becomes an art. Notwithstanding that it is unhealthy for man to know his fate, heaven's solicitude withholds it from him as much as ever possible. And there might be countless other technical causes for error.

The prophet, on the other hand, does not seek to know the future. It does not interest him. Nothing is of interest to him except that "he is consumed with the zeal of the house of God." He walks among men, no longer as a man, but as a formidable force—as the voice of the Almighty. He does not know what he cries in the wilderness, he is not concerned about it. His role is to desire, to be consumed, to inflame, to kindle everything around him. Intelligence, science, the deep motives of the leaders among men, and the ingenious patience of educators are not his concern. That is not his work. His work is to brandish the torch of God, from which little sparks fall upon the stooped and weary spines: he forces men to stand erect; he forces them to lift their mournful eyes to the heights. He speaks without awareness—yes, but it is God who speaks through him.

The Canticle of Zacharias

And God knows—that suffices. The eternal Spirit possesses the spirit of the prophet. He leads the prophet into the world of providential decrees. He makes him take the roads forbidden to other men. And, at intervals, the mouth repeats involuntarily, you might say, what the conscience has retained from these secret meetings between his soul and the angels. The prophet does not always see the scope of his foretellings; he does not lead a normal life. He offers the extraordinary spectacle of an unstable yet permanent equilibrium between the earthly stasis and the celestial stasis. The result being that his auditors understand something else than what he said, unless they too are with God. In short, he speaks beyond the mental level of the people; he is the magician at whose voice the impossible becomes possible, the imaginary becomes real, the hidden becomes manifest. Adepts, spirits of the elements, and gods produce soothsayers; God alone produces prophets.

The Canticle of Zacharias, similar to the one of the Virgin, is a hymn of praise in two parts. In the first part, the mercy of God is celebrated; in the second, the favors of the Savior. In it one sees the mechanism of collective spiritual life laid bare. As we have already stated, humankind wears itself out primarily to obtain privileges from the gods. We, however, are not concerned here with mere contacts of magic, but with the ordinary acts with which the weft of our existence is woven. The activities we make use of in the hope of satisfying our inner desires in reality become canalized towards the substantial kingdoms of the objective gods who rule each of these desires—and our many "me"s sign tacit pledges with these gods. We are shortsighted borrowers.

These gods, just like our earthly bankers, do not lend without interest. These interests compound. There comes a time when we cannot repay, and so we become the slaves of pitiless loan sharks. From that moment on, our spiritual fate is in jeopardy. Our spirit is really endangered, and no other powerful creature can aid us—that could only postpone the account due and further increase it. If the Father wishes to save us, he must draw from his treasure. Luckily, his treasure is bottomless. The indemnity offered by the Father to our spiritual creditors is the "redemption of his people" that Zacharias extols.

However, being indocile and stubborn, it is good for us to experience some of the harshness of our spiritual lenders. But having ceased to flatter them, we now call them enemies, since they make us suffer, and we revile them. And yet, it was when they were granting us their favors that they were really our enemies. Now that they make us work, they are actually rendering us a service: we should thank them. Heaven could forbid them from demanding payment of debts, but that would not be just. God reimburses them from his own funds; he liberates us while substituting himself in our stead.

That is why the Word took a physical body.

Outside of these enmities, which after all are normal and logical, there are certain beings who really hate us. But rare are the men to whom it is given to have real enemies. Those who appear to attack us through pure nastiness are really nothing but old creditors. The soldiers of heaven, alone, have authentic enemies, because only when we have almost acquitted ourselves of our personal debts can we be recruited into the army of light: then we are hated because of the king we serve. Beings are jealous of the man in

The Canticle of Zacharias

whom they feel a secret force on which they would like to feed. These beings are the followers of darkness, and the "soldiers" combat and conquer them by means of all-powerful kindness, while allowing themselves to be despoiled by them.

To the few who aspire to be recruited into this glorious and obscure militia, I will give a word of warning: the title of soldier is a heavy one to bear. We already find it painful to be obliged to repair the damage we have caused; we cry: injustice. This is but passive work, merely land-clearing. The plow must follow, and finally the seeding comes. The soldier is the shaft of corn that comes from the earth.

You have witnessed occasionally some passer-by annoying an animal in zoological gardens till the poor beast, irritated, jumps and growls while shaking the bars of its cage. We are just like these animals, locked behind bars of matter. And the genii of a superior race passing by excite us in order to amuse themselves at our powerlessness and at our anger. Then, a minute or two later, they go on.

That is exactly what is meant by these precise and terrible temptations of saints that sometimes last twenty-five years, as in the case of the venerable César de Bus. In the invisible, that length of time represents but the mere pause of a passer-by. And yet, these constant, faithful, courageous saints may not even be soldiers.

The soldier is not content to submit stoically to fatigue, hunger, or rain: he must also attack. But for him, attack means sacrificing himself; it means to spend and give of one's self without retaining anything; it means holding the same benevolent smile when confronted with ingratitude or hatred; it means converting self-pride, vanity, and the quite natural expectation of "value received" into total selflessness. It means that nothing can ever take us away from the kingdom of the Father or from that state of soul where only light, peace, and tenderness reign.

This martyrdom, which the soldier accepts for centuries, whose torments he undergoes with immutable serenity, lasts until the light has finally transmuted the darkness within these adverse beings. It is the great battle that began with the dawn of the world, the outcome of which was decided by the coming of Christ, and which will terminate only with the final triumph of our Lord.

Throughout all these inconceivable happenings we are comforted by the presence of the Master: a presence that, though usually invisible, seems completely withdrawn from us at times, and yet occasionally affirms itself through some physical realization. In fact, during the sequence of lives of a soldier, there are some blessed years when he fights with the support of his chief, in a physical body, by his side. This miracle occurs each time a free man takes one of us into his following. The free man is not the Word in person, yet he is the Word; he is one of the Word's new incarnations.

Such a one appears within humanity as a brilliant, pure cell that stops the decomposition of other cells, that cures them in every way, gives life back to them, who reorganizes, reassembles, and brings them back for the assault.

At intervals, upon all planets, descend "free men" in whose spirit the natural ascending lights are concentrated and in whom the supernatural descending lights meet.

There are several of them, yet they form but one spirit; they are the sparks, and their reunion is the dazzling body of the Word, the ordinator of the destinies of the universe. They alone to whom grace has been given will know and recognize them. Nobody merits that grace. To have received

The Canticle of Zacharias

it constitutes an extraordinary privilege, tasking those who have been awarded it with the heaviest of responsibilities. Because, though the free man passes unnoticed by those who do not belong body and soul to Christ, though his physical personality bears no identifying marks—neither the clairvoyance of a visionary nor the inquiry of an adept will ever discern him, unless he permits it. The light that such a being carries, though it remains impenetrable, is the very light of the eternal.

⊕

The last verses of the Canticle of Zacharias are addressed to the little Precursor. That which we have already mentioned regarding the spirit of this child proves that he was the Prophet par excellence.

His function, not only in his earthly life, but in the permanency of his spiritual life, is fourfold: he prepares the ways for the Lord; he brings salvation to men; he enlightens the blind; he leads them.

In order to understand this, one must know that, even before the beginning of time, Christ was the first act of the Father: in very truth the first-born. That is also why he remains the ever-sacrificed one. But the personality of Christ increases parallel with the growth of creation. It will be perfected only when creation will have exerted all its energies and completed its development also. That is the total sense in which the Word is the alpha and the omega.

Synchronously, by prodigious sacrifice, the worldwide growth of the Word remains subject to our goodwill: for it to be, we men must first of all desire it. He must prepare his pathways, and we also have to smooth out his ways. The Precursor is the model of this collective work.

There lies our salvation. Through it, alone, beatitude becomes accessible to us. This work is nothing but the fulfillment of the Father's will. This will is the selfsame biological law of nature. As each one of our infractions brings suffering and death upon us, it is necessary for heaven to intervene and for its mercy to annul the results of these infringements. That is what the remission of sins consists of.

Once the moral, spiritual, mental, or physiological evil has been lifted, heaven completes its work of healing by erecting a torch over our heads. The Precursor is the arm holding that torch. His labors, pains, and his very life are food to this flame. That living torch burns from unexplainable anguish in order to enlighten the crowds wallowing in the swamps. It is ablaze on the hillsides at night; and some people, lifting their hopeless eyes towards this brazier, find a desire being born within them to reach it. That is how his inner and outer, invisible and visible, psychic and physical martyrdom lifts us little by little to the heights from where we can finally see the peaceful city of the King and his eternal gardens.

But here the evangelist drops the veil upon these ineffable horizons and puts us face to face with the little child of Elizabeth. Exegetes pretend that these words, "He grew, and waxed strong in spirit, and was in the deserts till the day he manifested in Israel," hide the Essenian initiation of John the Baptist. This is an erroneous opinion. The one to whom "Jehovah is propitious" (that is the meaning of the name John, or Jochanan) has no further need of human wisdom, no matter how pure or lofty it may be.

"To grow in spirit" does not mean to augment one's psychic forces by more or less scientific methods. The forces that are developed within us by initiatory exercises—no

The Canticle of Zacharias

matter how subtle they are—do not belong to the spirit, but to substance. When the spirit grows in us, it is of its *own* accord, through the spontaneity of its nature—regardless of regimes and without any outside stimulations. The spirit grows automatically in proportion as our will (meaning the heart) becomes purified by renouncing itself.

But, according to the law, one must eat in order to grow. And the little John spent his youth in deserts, both figuratively and in the true sense. We must comprehend this in the broader and deeper meaning of the Scriptures. There are many kinds of deserts. The terrain from which the heavenly plants have been pulled out, no matter how fertile and rich it may be with nature's plants—the terrain where the brooks of grace do not flow—is still a desert to a soul such as the Baptist. It is an arid place, one of desolation, powerlessness, and even death.

Paris, London, Nineveh, and Chicago can be Saharas: the child of God does not recognize in the swarming multitude anyone reminding him of his native land. Note the extraordinary mode of heaven's activity. According to nature, anyone deprived of nourishment perishes. According to God, the missionary who receives nothing from this earth, but who, on the contrary, gives something ceaselessly, becomes sublimated, lives, and radiates through continents and worlds. The little Precursor, growing up far from civilization and human wisdom, is brought up by the Spirit alone. The majestic spectacles of the desert teach him all arcana. The dramas of solar light played out upon this immense state clothe his intelligence with beauty. With each new dawn, he prays for infinite hope; with each noon, he becomes exalted with the power overshadowing him; at dusk, he follows the slow descent of the solar-king behind noble hills, which brings to the surface of that young heart the ever-growing nostalgia for his spiritual land. At night, in contrast to the august peacefulness of nature, the child trained himself for invisible fights, internal contentions, and the secret trials that were preparing him for his public life.

May this adolescence be an example to us. We too, whatever be our destiny or work, let us think of the desert; let us seek it, and like it. Solitude is nourishment for the strong. Absence of human companions attracts the invisible; but psychic solitude irresistibly draws the angels of the divine Presence. And these were the visitors of the little John. For him the stars, torrents, shrubs, cacti, rank fig trees, birds, and wild beasts shed their form of matter. He could see their terrestrial spirit, and, tracing back step by step, he found the leaders who from the depths of mystical spaces administer universal life. He maintained himself in that rare state wherein, to the psychic, each being reveals itself according to eternal reality. That state is not inaccessible. There are quite a few contemporary examples of this, among whom was the Cure d'Ars, who, as he was conferring with the Virgin in his room one night, felt a pull on his sleeve. It was his servant who had walked in to tell him dinner was ready, and without surprise the candid saint turned around and in all innocence, said, "My Lord, is that you?" When will we become so preoccupied with heaven as to live thus with him?

John the Baptist was poor. He lived nearly naked and without a roof. But to him the skies were open, and their inhabitants tangible and familiar. That is true happiness: immutable, infinite, perpetual. May we also soon taste its first fruits!

Bethlehem

N THOSE DAYS there went out a decree from Caesar Augustus that a census be taken of all the world. This census was made while Cyrenius was governor of Syria. Thus, all went to register, each one in his own city. Joseph then went up from Galilee, out of the city of Nazareth, to Judea, into the city of David, which is called Bethlehem (because he was of the house and lineage of David), to be taxed with Mary, his espoused wife, who was with child. While they were there, the time that she should be delivered arrived. And she brought forth her first-born son, wrapped him in swaddling clothes and laid him in a manger because there was no room for them at the inn. (Luke 2:1–7; Matthew 1:18–25)

This was the unique event in the annals of the earth. The *event* par excellence. The fantastic fact upon which we should constantly focus the sight of our intelligence and of our love. It is the birth of Jesus, the birth of God.

Here we have to amass our attentive forces, order all the voices of our inner powers to keep still, and force our lordly selves, decked out in their "Sunday-best" garments, to get upon their knees. Otherwise our comprehension becomes warped, and any spiritual benefit annuls itself. Let us glance back and recapitulate the events we have studied up till now.

These events took place so that "the prophesied promise of the coming of a Savior would be fulfilled," says Matthew.

The Father binds himself through his prophets; he keeps his word no matter what—because of that part of us that has kept the memory of his word and expects its realization. He does not modify his projects; he simply changes the means whenever he deems it necessary—though he has already foreseen those changes.

He does not force anyone. His eventual collaborators, Joseph and Mary, had to remain free to accept his propositions and to repel the attempts of the Adversary. So, although the Father is total goodness, do not let yourself fall into quietism. It is only when we have done our utmost that heaven comes to our assistance.

So, let us look at the nativity from a fresh standpoint.

The mode of the maternity of the Virgin is unacceptable to science. Rigorously speaking, parthenogenesis does not exist in nature. Whenever it seemingly happens, it is because the paternal agent comes from a different plane than the one of the maternal agent. Demonological history abounds with such happenings. Yet, not only infrahuman beings can come into physical existence that way; also much higher beings than we are exceptionally use this process to descend to earth for a specific purpose; and this is possible even for creatures of other races than that of Adam.

That is why (in parenthesis) we should not condemn in our mind the criminal, because he may be a demon in the process of sanctifying himself. And neither should we glorify the hero, because the wake of glory he leaves behind him may not come from the world of pure light. We must look upon all creatures as workers of God.

But far be it from me to dare compare these "natural"

Bethlehem

phenomena of parthenogenesis to the "supernatural" miracle of the conception of Christ.

Our plan does not include notions of esoteric embryology, which could be stated here: in these pages, such elaborations would be needless and disrespectful. Suffice for us to know that, in order to contain the extreme activity of his spirit, Jesus needed a perfectly pure physical vessel; and to obtain this, the virginity of his mother was indispensable.

Here the guileless ardor of a St Francis of Assisi, the celestial palette of a Fra Angelico, the profoundly moving candor of a Verlaine, would be needed to describe the scene of the nativity. All is fresh, innocent, full of grace, like a primitive fresco on ancient Etrurian walls. No room here for hieratic teachings or metaphysics. The divine and the human, embracing each other, entirely fill the framework of our sensitivity, immobilize our intelligence, and throw into the very center of our will the darts of redeeming emotions by means of which the regenerating fires of love propagate.

The King of the gods simply comes down to earth, and his cradle is a manger, because there is no room at the inn. What terrible simplicity one finds in St Luke's gospel! How that sentence should make us blush with shame! Because that particular event still happens every day. Each day, at least once, the spirit of Jesus knocks at the door of the hostelry of our spirit, asking that we give him a part of ourselves, that he may be clothed and incarnated in it; but only once in a thousand times do we, mere dust and mire, extend to him a thought, a word, or a gesture. And then we are surprised when nature, indignant at our ingratitude, pours acid upon our selfishness, pounces upon our heart, and activates the fire under its crucibles.

THE CHILDHOOD OF JESUS

Look again at the harmony of the circumstances of the nativity in which a thousand meanders of providential designs are being resolved.

It was necessary that the Messiah be born in Bethlehem. This was the hamlet where the invisible roads ended, and where the crowded phalanxes of auxiliary genii merged. Mammon suddenly decided to take a census of his forces, the administrative machine of the Roman colossus started grinding, and the couple from Nazareth was obliged to leave for Jerusalem. Thus the omnipotent, self-satisfied Caesar prides himself at that very moment when the atom of supernatural energy (that one day will destroy him) instills itself into his monstrous body. One can imagine how a decree, launched by the Father, mobilizes in each of the worlds through which it passes the workers of destiny and the invisible stage-directors thanks to whom creatures accomplish the acts that fulfill divine will. The individual wills of beings can advance or retard only a little the epoch set by the Word. And so Christ, the living bread, is going to be born in Bethlehem: "the house of bread."[1] And we wit-

---

[1] May I be permitted to exhume for the sheer curiosity of the thing, a little-known theory that the Templars extracted from Celtic initiations and that the Rosicrucians of the seventeenth century borrowed: "The Word is the uncut stone that falls from the height of time down to the depths of space, through the ecliptic, thereby separating cosmic potential from the non-becoming. This was the first day, the *fiat lux*, the Beth-El. As it stops on its descent, becoming immobile before reascending, it is Beth-Il. As it reascends through the efforts of man, even though often erroneous, it is the flat stone, the house of lies, Beth-Aven. Finally, it reintegrates its point of departure. It becomes the cut and open cube, the stone that opens, the stone with the 144 sides, the cubic stone, the stone of life: Beth-Lehem."

Bethlehem

ness his inaugurating the method he will pursue during his entire existence as he chooses the most difficult conditions in which to perform all things.

This gives us the perfect model to follow in each similar circumstance; it encourages us, or rather it should give us a burning courage, were we attentive. After which, difficulties permit his using greater power.

Finally, his fatigue lightens our load in advance of the time when a similar effort will be asked of us.

The mission that Jesus set for himself is to sow in each of the countless meetings of feelings, of thoughts, of material and moral circumstances, a spark of his divine virtue—to incarnate himself within all states of soul, physical gestures, and intellectual enigmas, so that through our consent and collaboration, heaven may be realized and fulfilled on all earths.

Since Christ passed through the caverns of darkness, quagmires, and solitudes, their prestige of terror has been lost, and we are able to go through them with less pain, knowing ahead of time how we should behave so that the luminous emanations that Christ left in them may increase.

To operate his mission, he could have launched currents of healing forces or changed something in the machinery of the world; but he took the path where, if I may so put it, his person had to pay the most: his incarnation.

When he incarnated, he might have chosen a rich and powerful family in a dominant country; instead, he chose a people enslaved, chose the least cultured of tribes (Galileans being looked down upon by other Jews) and a poor family without a decent abode. He has done the same thing in every circumstance, and if someone wants to be his friend, he must imitate him.

THE CHILDHOOD OF JESUS

From the cosmogonic standpoint, the first seven verses of the second chapter in Luke could serve us as groundwork for vast developments. In the Old Testament, for example, take the Books of Moses, of Kings and Judges, the Psalms, Ecclesiastes, and the Song of Solomon—they relate the preparatory period of creation, the collective effort of beings choosing an elect, symbolized by Israel, which by its vigor organizes flowing currents, calls beings, and prepares the ways according to unity—so that, from the relative standpoint, the descent of the Messiah may become possible. In the bosom of this elect, a branch, the one of David, has the mission of engendering the unique and immaculate flower who will be the mother of the Messiah.

Then begins the veritable life of the world, whose tale unfolds throughout the four gospels up to the apocalyptic coronation. The Word manifests in the terrestrial body of the celestial Virgin, which means: first he is born on a planet without fanfare, without glory; and only afterward will he propagate himself in the totality of created planes. He is born in the middle of the night, in winter, when the tired universe is in lethargy, at a time when the prince of this world (Caesar) thinks he has won the victory and organizes his forces. The only witnesses to the accomplishment of the mystery are the mother (manifested nature), who remains a virgin[2] after this particular birth, the apparent father (energy of evolution), the ox (symbol of fructifying forces), and the donkey (symbol of effort)—these three latter being the three radical energies found on any plane of existence.

Should I mention here the symbolic interpretations invented by men? St Gregory of Nyssa and St Augustine

---

[2] As theology and liturgy teach it.

Bethlehem

have spoken of the solar myth long before Volney and Dupuis. Long before astrologers and alchemists, Prudence informed us that this nativity would cause the renewal of all things. And since, as one sings in an noble old hymn "...the Incarnation took place so that knowing God in a visible form, through him we will be ravished for love of invisible things...," I will not bother to enumerate all scholarly calculations.³ I will merely indicate a few avenues that the liturgical forms open to the mind of the student.

In the first centuries, Christians spent the entire Christmas eve in prayer. Shortly after, they began to celebrate it with three masses: the midnight one, in honor of the earthly birth of the Word; the one at dawn, in honor of his inner birth within our spirit; and the one of the day, in honor of his eternal generation in God. This march indicates the progression itself of our experiential knowledge of Christ. The three nocturnes of the matins of Christmas recalls the three ages of the creation of the world: up to Moses, from Moses to Christ, and from Christ until the end of time. Formerly, at the moment of the second nocturne, the pope would bless a helmet and a sword that he would later send to some great Catholic captain, because the fifth lesson of this nocturne mentions the battle Christ had to fight against evil in order to incarnate.

---

³ According to Kepler, the nativity occurred between 747 and 750 of the Roman calendar; in any case, not after April 740. The Eastern Church has successively celebrated Christmas on January 6 and May 15; the Church of Antioch chose December 25 in 376 (St Clement of Alexandria and St John Chrysostom). According to the visionary Mary of Agreda, one would say December 25, 5199 at midnight (or rather, December 25, 749); and finally, tradition has fixed it at Friday, December 25, 747 (Baronious).

THE CHILDHOOD OF JESUS

⊕

And there were in the same country shepherds abiding in the field, keeping watch over their flocks by night. And, lo, the angel of the Lord came upon them, and the glory of the Lord shone round about them: and they were filled with fear. The angel said to them, Fear not: for, behold, I bring you good tidings of great joy, which shall be to all people. For unto you is born this day, in the city of David, a Savior, who is Christ the Lord. And this shall be a sign unto you: Ye shall find the babe wrapped in swaddling clothes, lying in a manger. And suddenly there was with the angel a multitude of the heavenly host, praising God, and saying: Glory to God in the highest, and peace on earth to men of goodwill. Then it came to pass as the angels were gone away from them into heaven, the shepherds said one to another, Let us now go into Bethlehem, and see this thing which is come to pass, which the Lord has made known to us. So they came with haste and found Mary and Joseph, and the babe lying in a manger. And when they had seen him, they made known abroad the saying which was told them concerning this child. And all they that heard it wondered at those things which were told them by the shepherds. But Mary kept all these things, and pondered them in her heart. And the shepherds returned, glorifying and praising God for all the things that they had heard and seen as it was told unto them. (Luke 2:8–20)

The apparition of the angel to the shepherds is nothing out of the ordinary: the various modes of universal life are closely interwoven, and no movement occurs even in the farthest plane of the invisible without some reaction setting in to our physical plane, and vice versa. It follows that an event as grave as the birth of Christ would have remarkable repercussions. Phenomena of this order are neither auto-suggestions, hallucinations, nor the result of physiological depressions. In any event, hallucinations do not exist in the sense used by medical men, because perception never takes place without some objective reality. In the case at hand, it is not the spirit of the spectator that moves about; it is the spectacle that comes to him, whether it be that a scene, a summary portrayal of the invisible, descends over him, or else a veil is drawn aside. In fact, we live, as it were, in rooms where drapes that separate these various apartments are drawn aside only when we give proof of being able to utilize the lesson that will be shown, or when there is urgency.

These apartments communicate: a nation, a family, an idiom, an epoch are all groups constituting rooms therein. The perception of the summary portrayal or its comprehension, visually as well as auditively, results from a spontaneous adaptation of the beings that animate it; and on a higher level, it is analogous to the means we employ to make ourselves understood by a stranger. In any case, the messengers heaven sends us always have sufficient knowledge and power to make their words very clear.

The peace wished to men of goodwill by the host of angels who offered themselves to the service of the newborn Jesus is the emanation, the wake, the atmosphere of Christ. This peace is one of the forms of the Holy Spirit. The Trinity is an aspect of God revealed to man to help his intelligence, but none of the three Persons are ever separated: the Father is always there where the Son acts, and the Spirit is always the result—the link, may I say, to their simultaneous presence. That is why peace is the sign of the action of the

Spirit. It is the absence of strife, it is harmony, and equilibrium. It cannot exist without the perfect collaboration of all parts of the whole. Hence, it is engendered by the sacrifice of the individual for the collectivity—and it is love that confers upon it the power to accomplish this sacrifice.

From the cosmogonic sense, the Christian kabbalists say that the shepherds represent the fragments of the third form of universal humanity, that of Ram-Adam, and that the confused multitude of these fragments, erring here and there at random in their state of darkness, have been reanimated, reassembled, and reorganized by the coming of the Messiah. (Rabbi Isaac Loria)

Yes, yes, but how consoling is the angel's wish: "Peace on earth to men of goodwill!" A wish proffered by very pure mouths receives the force of realization. Since the time of Jesus, in fact, men of goodwill enjoy the peace of God. They may suffer from enemies and tempests as others do, but peace dwells among them in spite of all. However, the goodwill that animates them is far from the good intentions that pave the road to hell, as one is told. According to gospel terminology, everything is understood from the standpoint of totality. And the goodwill that the angels mention is not merely a fugitive exuberance that spurts here and there during the course of an existence: it is a constant, permanent, inflexible tension. Besides, it is not merely good occasionally, or up to a certain height; it is simply, unanimously, and all-encompassingly Good. True goodwill, in fact, is represented as a simple unity. The two qualities blend: that which is simple, is a unity; that which is a unity, is total. A man of goodwill wants to do good from his heart, his intelligence, and through his body. He realizes the unity he adores in his infinitely small capacity, but nevertheless he

Bethlehem

does realize it. That is why shepherds, who were simple men, were taught by angels; while magi, who were complicated men, were only forewarned by a sign.

And this goes on day after day.

⊕

The shepherds relate the marvelous apparition. When should miracles be disclosed? When should they be kept quiet? All truths are not to be divulged, and charity demands prudence. If you take poor shepherds away from their pastures into the midst of luxury with the intention of giving them all possible happiness, do you not run the risk of heading them towards drunkenness and debauchery? If you transport an uncultivated brain into a circle of high intellectuality, where one plays with ideas as easily as acrobats juggle, the poor man will certainly lose his energy of action and you will have made a derelict of him. "Be as wise as serpents," says the Master. We do not know our neighbors; a notion acceptable to one, beneficial for the second, is merely toxic for the third. And evil is always greater for the mind than for the body.

If the invisible reveals itself to you, and if it does not order you to publish it, keep your experiences private, for you and yours. If you are to broadcast it, it will clearly advise you to do so. Our mission, to us common among mortals, is to act by example, which is already a very difficult task—yet it is the only mode of profitable teaching of which we are capable. The word of an apostle, in order to be alive, demands that this apostle have prepared himself by incarnating his ideal through all sorts of works; and we are far from having accomplished that task.

That is why the Virgin was satisfied with "conserving in

THE CHILDHOOD OF JESUS

her heart" the remembrance of the marvels she had witnessed. She will only mention them much later to the chosen elite among the disciples. Today, twenty centuries of culture later, seeing how few men accept and understand miracles, the contemporaries of Christ may well be excused for not having accepted them.

When Jesus was born at Bethlehem, in Judea, in the days of King Herod, from the East there came wise men to Jerusalem, saying, Where is he that has been born, King of the Jews? We have seen his star in the East and have come to worship him. When King Herod had heard these things, he was troubled and all Jerusalem with him. So he assembled all the chief priests and scribes of the people together, inquiring of them where Christ was to be born. And they said to him: At Bethlehem in Judea; for thus it has been written by the prophet: And thou Bethlehem, of the land of Juda art not the least among the principal cities of Juda, for out of thee shall come a Governor that shall rule my people Israel. Then Herod, summoning the wise men in secret, inquired of them at what exact time the star had appeared, then he sent them to Bethlehem, saying: Go and search diligently for the young child and when you have found him, bring me word so that I may go and worship him also. When they had heard the king, they went on their journey; and all at once the star which they had seen in the East went before them till it stood still directly over where the young child was. When they saw the star, they rejoiced

Bethlehem

beyond measure. Going into the dwelling, they found the young child with Mary his mother, and fell to their knees and worshipped him; and after they had opened their treasures, they presented to him gifts: gold, frankincense and myrrh. Being warned of God in a dream that they should not return to Herod, they departed to their own country by another way. (Matthew 2:1–12)

The Church celebrates the Adoration of the Magi on January 6, under the name of Epiphany, and on the same day it commemorates the wedding of Cana. Thus it groups together the traditional filiation of Christ, according to human wisdom, with his divine filiation and his first miracle, model of all others: a transmutation according to the Spirit of this world, and a regeneration according to the divine Spirit. This feast is called Theophany or Feast of Lights in the Greek rite. It was on that day that baptisms were performed during the first centuries.

The Syrian and Armenian liturgies claim there had been twelve magi; the Catholic liturgy names only three: Melchior, of the race of Shem, king of Arabia or Iran; Caspar, of the race of Ham, king of Sheba or Ethiopia; and Balthazar, of the race of Japheth, king of Tharsis (Ceylon). When you realize that "Arab" comes from the root word meaning "the West," that Sheba means "conversion" or "captivity," and that Tharsis means "contemplation of joy," one discovers three antinomies between these meanings and the gifts offered the God-child. In effect, Melchior offers gold: symbol of royalty; Caspar offers incense: symbol of prayer and divinity; Balthazar offers myrrh: symbol of suffering.[4]

---

[4] *Missel de Paris*, sixteenth century.

THE CHILDHOOD OF JESUS

Let us add to these notes that in the Old Testament the magi-kings were prefigured by Abel, Seth, and Enosh; then by Shem, Ham, and Japheth; finally by Abraham, Isaac, and Jacob. St John Chrysostom states that much later they were baptized by St Thomas. This apostle, whose name might indicate the twin, the double, the Janus, the abyss, and the doubter, represents, according to Hermetic interpretation, to which the gospel is susceptible, human wisdom, which is twice dual: exoteric or esoteric; experiential or speculative. In order to convince himself, later, St Thomas had to touch with his finger the wound on the side, or the fifth door of the Word, after which he went to preach in India, the country of secret sciences. To him, the resurrection seemed impossible, because he possessed certain knowledge of esoteric physiology.

A lot of trouble has been taken to identify the star of the magi. Some believe it was the comet that the Chinese observed for seventy days in 748. Kepler, Ideler, Schubert, and Pfaffe claim that it was formed by the extraordinary conjunction of Saturn with Jupiter, Mars, Venus, and Mercury in the Roman years of 747 or 748. Others assimilate it with the star of the Rosicrucians that appeared in the constellation of the Serpent Bearer in 1604—at the same time as the conjunction of Saturn with Mars. Still others think it to have been Halley's comet. But what is certain is that the whole East, warned by their oracles, were awaiting something (cf. Tacitus and Suetonius).

The Koran (3:34) considers this star as the material sign of the coming of Aissa (Jesus), John the Baptist being its spiritual sign. Beha Ullah, the second pontiff of Bahaism, affirms that such a star appears each time there is a divine manifestation, and that it is both material and spiritual.

Bethlehem

In closing this series of information, let us notice, from the geogenic standpoint, that if Herod is the representative of the prince of this world, the shepherds are the unknown and unsung servants of heaven, and the magi-kings represent the kindly gods.

Really, nothing precise is known about those mysterious kings or about their stellar guide. They wear the aureola of incognito. But the real lesson they teach us is, as said above, that, being astrologers, these scholars were called by a star; and they have the dual merit of having come from afar and of not having been blinded by their knowledge, whereas the Jews, who were close by, did not bother coming over, nor did the doctors of the Synagogue care to accept the evidence of the Messianic texts.

According to prophecies, the scribes told Herod that Bethlehem was to be the natal city of the Messiah. All that which is to happen some day on earth exists already in the invisible—in fact, since the beginning of the world. Certain men at rare intervals are able to get a glimpse into this enclosure where all the essential forms of terrestrial events are assembled. In certain cases their brain, activated by certain elemental spirits for just that purpose, enlists mental processes to translate into terrestrial language this mysterious spectacle that their spirit witnessed.

In prophecies, places are always clearly defined, but not the dates. There are several reasons for such apparent anomalies. First of all, a prophecy is nothing but an anticipatory sign for those who will be able dutifully to face the event, and is illegible for the others.

The invisible schemas of events, the configurations, follow certain paths in the beyond, and those paths are immutable. But the wayfarers walk either slowly or fast. The invisible road corresponds to the terrestrial sites; the state of the guiding pattern determines the moment of its realization. Yet, those patterns can be modified in all of their premises. We must be satisfied with this simple analogy because, for a more complete explanation, it would be necessary to understand the essence of time and space. We, however, are not yet wise enough to shoulder the responsibilities such knowledge would put upon us.

Nothing is inevitable: one minute before a thing may happen, heaven can change it. Yet there are some providential designs that God has not modified since the beginning of the world. Thus, divination is in vain, because it is human, limited in its concepts, impatient, and small in its means. But God, when he thinks it necessary, has his prophets speak in order to give us hope, to sow the seeds of a new creation, or to set some creatures going. Hence, let us wait in patience, confidence, and with awareness of mind.

⊕

Let us look at the invisible origin of the idea of gifts, as we study the gifts the magi brought the child Jesus. In creation, it is automatically the lesser who receives from the higher. In the uncreated, each gives himself to all others perpetually. Hence, the disciple of Christ must return the fruits of his works to his Master; but as creatures are in need of it also, the offering to the Lord remains solely in the motive.

That which the magi brought are nothing but the outer sign of their real offerings and of their sentiments. The magi presented precious gifts. The shepherds brought noth-

Bethlehem

ing but their hearts. In fact, there are, from the standpoint of our relationship with God, two kinds of men: those who believe themselves to be centers and who are aware of their value, and those who believe themselves to be worthless. The first offer nothing but a part of the share of their work; or if nothing more, they keep their own little selves aside. The latter, by contrast, never think of retaining any benefit from their efforts. They are selfless; they have accomplished the supreme sacrifice of human liberty: to become the slaves of God. And because God is perfect liberty, in this "servitude" these slaves find infinite freedom.

I invite all of you to relive this scene of the nativity from time to time; you will experience better the vigorous lessons contained in it. All extremes seem to have met at a rendezvous: all-powerfulness met with the bereft; present incognito with future universal glory; angels with the stars; kings with the shepherds; and finally, the most incomprehensible mystery with the simplest incident of birth.

Christmas is the feast most erroneously celebrated. What is it even for the best people, but some kind of selfish joy? Spiritual selfishness, of course, but selfishness nonetheless. May at least a few Christians remember how sad that day must have been for the little child with the profound eyes: he was seeing all that he had undergone, and he was aware of all that he would still have to undergo. May this idea incite us, during the Christmases that God still grants us to live through, that instead of rejoicing, we may lighten the load which, from his first hour, crushed the delicate shoulders of the newborn in Bethlehem.

The Presentation

 HEN EIGHT DAYS had passed for the circumcising of the child, he was called Jesus, which is the name that was given by the angel before he was conceived in the womb of his mother. (Luke 2:21)

The God-child begins his terrestrial life by obeying: he submits to rites. What is a rite? It is a religious ceremony through which the spirit of the faithful receives a force analogous to the prescribed gestures and to the prescribed words, and that is determined by them. A rite, as any law, is a fence, or rather a path between two fences. It is a school, the school where one learns how to be the least detrimental to any other creatures. It is a gymnastic, a training in obedience that finally results in the possession of liberty.

In the books of magic, too widely prevalent today, one finds the theory of rites: the evocation of the superior by the sacrifice of the lesser. All liturgies are magical. But the Catholic sacraments possess something beyond that: the supernatural virtue that Jesus placed within their form and in their matter. We will take this up later.

Jesus, Mary, and Joseph are three pure beings. Consequently they are free, though on different levels. And yet they submit to the law. Why? First of all, to fulfill the law. To fulfill means to bring it up to perfection, to bring it to the very end of its trajectory, to bring it to fruition and to

The Presentation

complete its terrestrial action; in short, to deliver us from its chains—since any force, having achieved its terrestrial work in full, goes on to another training place. Also, these three persons obey so that their contemporaries will not see them as exceptional beings, and so they will not be scandalized. Finally, they pave the way for us to obey more easily, and for our liberty to be more easily obtained This is one application of the divine law of love: that the innocent pays for the guilty.

Circumcision is a form of initiation, a baptism of blood. Moses saw in it something else than a hygienic precaution. And the baptism of water is not to teach cleanliness to babies either. Moses had to organize a guard for monotheism by linking the Israelites to the celestial principle of action, to the positive and creative aspect of the Absolute. By cutting off a piece of unnecessary flesh from the body, the rabbi was cutting off from the spirit tendencies towards false gods. Just so, our priests, by pouring water over the head of the newborn, claim to wash the original sin from his soul and to annul the effects of corruption by depositing salt on his tongue. Rabbis, priests, imams, and brahmans all follow the old example of the hierophants who, standing between the visible and the invisible, had become able to realize on this side, that which their hands were operating on the other side.

But we, who feel that something else exists beyond magic, we surmise that rituals are but symbols interlinked; they are necessary because they lead to the holy liberty of love that man can attain only through the ways of justice. A law is nothing but a guardrail. One has to lean on it in order to be able to hold firm later against the vertigo of unfathomable depths. Then the guardrails will fall of their own accord. In the country where marauders are unknown, fields do not have hedges, nor doors locks.

In all the ancient civil and religious codes, primogeniture implies dignity, duties, and prerogatives; so does the masculine sex. Folklore proves the existence of such particularities even among savage tribes. In fact, the fulfilling forces of action belong to the male sex: it is woman who receives intuition; it is man who bodies it forth. Woman is physically passive and spiritually active; man is inwardly passive and outwardly active. On the other hand, in the ontological circulus of soul, there are some who are coming here for the first time: they are strangers who bring extra-earthly elements, and whose office completes and crowns the evolutionary effort. If, however, the same beings were to return repeatedly upon our planet, humankind, after having reached their ultimate, could not progress any more. Just as there are some individuals who at death leave this earth forever, there are others who bring to us a force, an idea, and unknown lights. And in order that these may reach fruition, it is essential that their heralds be the firstborn of couples, thanks to whom they embody on earth. And as the male sex is the best fitted for material work, one perceives the reason of the prestige generally attributed to it. And so, Christ, in his human nature, was the Firstborn; so was he also in his divine nature, since he is the Word also.

The name of Jesus, as indicated by the angel, is the very same name pronounced by the Father from the beginning. It contains all the properties of the Word, and it would explain them to us, were it in our domain to understand names. I cannot enter into the technical details: they belong to the esoteric domain—where I promised not to enter. Anyhow, all hieroglyphic commentaries one could give

The Presentation

would never exhaust but a minute part of that name. Were we to study it intellectually, we would reach nothing but its deformed reflections. To employ it willfully would be committing a sacrifice, since one would be imprisoning part of the Spirit, since one would be giving to individualism what belongs to love. One should never use that name but in the spontaneous enthusiasm of adoration, so that it may never be prostituted and that it may exalt us instead of throwing us down into the wells of the abyss.

When the days of her purification, according to the law of Moses, were accomplished, they brought the child to Jerusalem to present him to the Lord, as it is written in the law of the Lord: Every firstborn male that openeth the womb shall be called holy to the Lord, so they had to offer a sacrifice according to that which is said in the law of the Lord: a pair of turtledoves or two young pigeons.

There was a man in Jerusalem whose name was Simeon; the same man was just and devout, and waiting for the consolation of Israel. The Holy Spirit was upon him, and it had been revealed to him by the Holy Spirit that he should not meet death until he had seen the Christ whom the Lord had anointed. He now came led by the Spirit into the temple; and when the parents brought in the child Jesus to perform the custom according to the law, he took him in his arms and blessing God, said: Lord, now let thy servant depart in peace, according to your word; for my eyes have seen your salvation, which thou hast prepared in the sight of all people, this light to enlighten the Gentiles, and the glory of thy people Israel. Joseph and his mother marveled at those things which were spoken of him. Simeon blessed them, and said to Mary, his mother, Behold, this child is destined to bring about the fall of many and the rise of many in Israel; to be a sign which shall be spoken against; and so the thoughts of many hearts may be revealed. Yea, a sword shall pierce through thy own soul also. There was also a prophetess, named Anna, the daughter of Phanuel, of the tribe of Aser; she was advanced in years, as she had lived with a husband seven years from her virginity; and had been a widow for about eighty-four years. She abode in the temple night and day and served God with fastings and prayers. She, too, coming in that instant, likewise gave thanks unto the Lord, and spoke of the child to all them that awaited for the redemption of Israel. And when they had performed all things according to the law of the Lord, they returned to Galilee, to their own city of Nazareth. (Luke 2:22–39)

The Feast of the Purification was instituted as an antidote to the Roman Lupercalia feasts. It is also known as the "Procession of Lights" or "Candlemas" day (February 2). It takes place in the second month of the year, which proves that it is linked to the being that some mystics have called the eternal Wisdom (Sophia). That is why Cardinal de Berulle calls that day the "Feast of the Secrets of God."

In our religion, the "churching of woman" (that is, the giving of thanks for the birth of a child) is performed according to the following rites. The mother presents herself at the church or at the chapel steps on her knees, holding a lighted candle. The priests come towards her reciting the

The Presentation

Psalm "Glory to the Lord"; then he leads her to the altar, while having her hold the left extremity of his white stole. The left is the passive side: the septentrion. Creatures come out of the right side of the cosmic Word, and re-enter heaven by his left side, through his heart, so as to be placed on his right side again after being dissolved in him. The priest prays with the woman that she may be freed from evil and from the sin of iniquity, so that she may obtain peace through the intercession of the Virgin. It is a fact that among all women the Virgin-Mother was the only one who did not need purification, since she had never been sullied. That is why she is all powerful as purificatrix. Finally, the priest blesses the bread the woman has baked with her own hands.

Under the Mosaic law, the period of purification lasted for forty days after the birth of a boy, and for eighty days after the birth of a girl. The offering had to be a pigeon for her, and a lamb for him: an easy symbol to fathom. But the fact of a double purification for a female child denotes, no more than the purification itself, anything unfavorable to women, a priori. In all exterior religions, in fact, parturition brings taints along with it. A child is not born without considerable labor on the part of the mother's vital spirit—physical pains are proofs thereof. The mother must hasten towards the child, because just as the shores of an ocean are always encumbered with refuse and meerschaum, the flowing, volatile ocean that surrounds the earth is inhabited on its borders by venomous, vampiric creatures whose covetousness is awakened by the approach of human spirits and physiological forces. The spirit of the mother cannot escape from these unclean contacts, and neither can the spirit of the child, especially if it is a female body that is prepared for it.

THE CHILDHOOD OF JESUS

⊕

The forty days of the Christmas season end with the feast of the Presentation of Jesus in the Temple, which the Greeks call the Feast of the Meeting, because of the elder Simeon. Simeon means "the listener," "the expectant one." The evangelist describes him as old and just: the dual qualities inherent to the one who knew that to wait also means "making it come." We moderns, sons of a hectic generation, should often meditate upon this figure whose grandeur is hidden.

Anna and Simeon were the second ones to know the true identity of the child. They received that information through a direct influx of the spirit. In fact, the unfathomable sacrifice of the Absolute making himself relative, the infinite limiting himself, the almightiness shouldering all chains, are concepts beyond the limits of our intelligence. There is no reasoning that can prove the divinity of Christ; there is no palpable testimony to certify it. To know it is a gratuitous gift. Among those who have had, at least once, the happiness of being in the presence of the Master, are to be found the elect to whom the Spirit revealed that this man was to be the consolation and the salvation of Israel.

The incarnation of the Word is not only (as pantheists teach) the diffusion of the divine among creatures: it is not a man of the elite being overshadowed by God. In Jesus, the Word dwells in all his plenitude. He is the Word, as well as the perfect Man. This belief, though rare, is still but an imprecise idea, a remote intuition that the future will develop. But that is sufficient for the work we have to do.

Christ is the salvation brought to all peoples and the light who is to enlighten all nations. He is "presented," not imposed upon peoples that are natural collective organ-

The Presentation

isms. He "must enlighten," not immediately but later, all nations that are artificial collective organisms. He offers himself to the first; he adapts himself to the second. His power is limitless; but he moderates its influx through his indulgence for the rebellious, by compassion for weaknesses, by patience for laziness. He took upon himself the chains of space and time—from his coming until his triumphant return. He submitted to the slow process of natural evolution. He placed himself within the confines of the law of matter, just as he stoops without impatience to the level of the most backward among us.

The world does not understand him and sees him only in the measure it desires to see him. This vision is increasing in intensity, clarity and scope, yes—but it is up to men to make it so. He is always ready to give himself to everything and to all of us if only we call him.

Israel represents the elect, though it really possesses nothing but what the Messiah gives it. That is why the Messiah is its glory. Evolution does not come wholesale, but grows in successive clusters. For example, when a particular race has ended its work, it leaves the earth definitively, in order to rest temporarily in some kind of paradise—while those of its members who have not satisfied the law go elsewhere to atone for their negligence. So, whenever a Savior unites his followers, the light that shines over them, the halo of their good works, does not come from them, but from him, because it is he who has given them the occasion and the power of accomplishing these works. Their merit is not one of having acted, but that of not having resisted the exhortation of their guide. That is how Christ is the glory of his people. His people have done for him only that which he gave them the means to do.

I do not mean to imply that we must await passively in quietude. We must make efforts, the greatest number of efforts possible, even those that seem impossible, because our acts are not real acts, they are counterfeits: we do not possess what is real, since we do not possess truth. When we believe that we can freely will, it is almost always because the impulse came from without. Our most heroic attempts are but outward signs of our desires. The child who stands tiptoe cannot reach the fruit, but his mother, seeing him stretch his little body, lowers the branch to the level of his hands. That is what Jesus does for us. The more we exercise our arms, the more they develop; and a day will come when we will have attained our stature as a man. That is the reason we should keep on trying.

Christ is an occasion for the fall and for the rising again of many, according to the inner state of each. In the heterogeneous mass, he acts as the supernatural reagent whose virtue separates the pure from the impure. "Birds of a feather flock together." The beings of light, even temporarily lost, go to the light; the beings of darkness, even if they appear to be luminous, go to darkness.

Just as artisans of the same craft live in the same neighborhood of a city, in the invisible, spirits meet according to their work and qualifications. The man of genius who appears in the middle of a troubled epoch resuscitates enthusiasm and hatred. His presence is like a spiritual cry: "You who love me, follow me!" Thus, the presence of Jesus draws to him those who have some spiritual kinship with him, and it repels the others. That is part of his judgment: spontaneous, without argument, formality, or inquest; a sentence that is a reclassification, a reorganization, a reconstruction.

The Presentation

Christ by his very self incites his own enemies because an action provokes a reaction, and those who are shocked by good do evil because of the presence of good. The contradiction that he and his friends are always facing intensifies the battle. I have seen such of his friends at close range. One would think that they liked to provoke contradiction, but they are doing right. For battle is movement, and movement is life. Man is still too backward to act by duty, by obedience, or for the love of God. He needs stimulants to get started. These stimulants are like rattles, toys of passion, and potions of covetousness. It would be better were he to work harmoniously, but rather than to remain idle it is even better for man to act with violence. Any effort spent in one direction makes the person capable of accomplishing another in the opposite direction; the deeper we become enmired, the higher summit do we crave. So, let us not fear obstacles. They will always remain proportionate to our strength—and that much more beneficial because their overthrow exacts the sacrifice of our personal inclinations.

The inner thoughts of a man's heart are discovered by the Messiah, because he is the splendor of truth. Evil and shadow cohabit on all planes (they engender each other), while truth, kindness, beauty—in short, light—dissipate all shadows. It is almost impossible for an irritated man not to reveal his real character. All beings reveal themselves when they are crossed in the natural course of events. Thus, the fight which the presence of Christ determines in the midst of the visible and invisible crowds he goes through has the logical effect of tearing away the veil of ruse of lies and hypocrisy.

Regarding the turmoil of truth that Jesus provokes, it is

he who feels its first whiplash with frightful pains. We cannot imagine the extent of his sensitivity. The more evolved an organism, the more delicate it is. Christ is reached by the movements of all his creatures. Nothing happens in the universe that he does not see; not a wound, but that it makes him bleed; not a tear shed, but that he tastes its bitterness. Yet all that beings take from him is still nothing, since his life is the constant sacrifice. His veritable martyrdom is to feel the multitude going to the shadows, those who tarnish his light and spend their lives—which lives he gave them—in evil. Yet Jesus obstinately remains in this martyrdom because he only wants to conquer through kindness, indulgence, and love.

And so, a friend shares the suffering of his friend. The servants of God are martyrs also. The closer they are to Jesus, the more they suffer. The Virgin, the first among these servants, justifies the old man's warning: "And even a sword will pierce your heart"; and moreover, she is the innocent among all innocents. Far are we from attaining her capacity for pain! Our sorrows are nothing but bruises—she, she was wounded unto death. And just think of the tortures before the final stroke!

There is little left for us to tell about Anna, the prophetess. Her life of solitude, fasts, and prayers, her education at the hands of the venerable rabbis, successors of the seventy initiates of Moses, had permitted her to read clearly into the obscure meanings of old texts. The Kabbalah does not contain the whole of truth; but the version it presents to the sincere and patient seeker is quite satisfactory.

Let us observe how prudent the prophetess was. She only speaks of the Messiah to those who are concerned with the salvation of Israel. One needs great discretion when one

The Presentation

deals with great truths. And I cannot repeat this too often—at a time when all men teach and when everyone writes—that a premature light becomes a poison. Good example is the finest sermon.

The Word

T THE BEGINNING of time was the Word, and the Word was abiding with God; and the Word was God. He was in the beginning of time with God. It was through him that all things came into being; and without him came nothing that has been made. In him was life, and the life was the light of all people. The light shines in the darkness, and the darkness did not overcome it. There appeared a man sent from God, whose name was John. He came as a witness to testify to the light, so that all might believe through him. He himself was not that light, but he came to testify to the light. The true light, which enlightens everyone, was coming into the world. He was in the world, and the world came into being through him; yet the world did not know him. He came to what was his own, and his own people did not accept him. But to all who received him, who believed in his name, he gave power to become children of God, who were born, not of blood (matter) or of the will of the flesh (nature) or of the will of man, but of God. And the Word was made flesh and lived among us, and we have seen his glory, the glory as of the only-begotten of the Father, full of grace and truth. (John testified to him and cried out, "This was he of whom I said, he who comes after me ranks ahead of me because he was before me.'") Of his abundance, we

The Word

have all received, grace upon grace. The law indeed was given through Moses; but grace and truth came through Jesus Christ. No one has ever seen God. It is God the only Son, who is close to the Father's heart, who has made him known. (John 1:1–18)

John's gospel differs from the other three in that the historical narrative is very brief. However, legend has taken hold of it, as well as of its author, probably because the mystery of the dual nature of Jesus is explained more fully in its effects therein than in the other texts.

In general, people attribute a beneficial property to the first chapter of this gospel. The truth is that, as it delineates the most exact description of the relationships between the divinity and its works, popular intuition supposes that these verses are saturated with some of the universal vital force and with the law, and that thereby the invisible beings who hear them being pronounced bow at the recollection of these primordial mysteries.

On the other hand, metaphysicians have erected upon John's statements quite a number of systems, some of which have earned uncontested glory for their authors. This doctrine finds its prefigurations in the I-Ching, in the Vedas, in the Druidic Triads, in the most ancient hieroglyphics of Egypt, America, and Assyria. I repeat: its *prefigurations*, because the sacred monuments of ancient times are susceptible of receiving the most diverse glosses, depending upon the standpoint of the reader. Finally, you will find deformations of the gospel doctrine, which are more or less obvious in the works of the Orientalists, when taking another look at Plato, Philo, or the Church Fathers.

If I take the liberty of belittling some of the sublime speculations of the philosophical mind, I do not imply that

THE CHILDHOOD OF JESUS

I will give you the exact sense of the text we are going to study. I do so only to show you how far man wanders from truth; to prove to you our intellectual weakness; to explain that, if it is right to render human masters all the esteem due them, one must not forget either that they were but men capable of error—that their greatest works are but provisional syncretisms; that if we really want to advance, our intellect must not permit itself to become fascinated by anything; that no matter how lofty our conception might be, we can be certain that it is but the inconclusive shadow of a still more magnificent idea.

We must first learn the lessons of the past to utilize them to illuminate the future, to know that everything is in a state of evolution, even the world of pure idea. We must learn these lessons in order to understand that we are still children; that we differ from one another; that all opinions, and the various ways of feeling and acting, have some worth. Thus will our intellectual sphere extend, and we will retain most of the teachings so profusely given to us by nature.

The Word is neither an abstraction nor an etheric ocean: the Word is a being: *the* Being. He and the other two Persons of the Christian Trinity constitute an indivisible, homogeneous whole, from which the ternaries of other theogonies (or religious beliefs) are particular points of view. In the Trinity, the Word is the expression closest to our intelligence, because, while the latter functions within the framework of the relative states, within the realms of matter, the Word himself is the vivificator of matter. What we conceive of the Absolute is, principally, the attributes of the Son.

The Word

What we conceive of the Son is his image refracted within the more or less dense strata of cosmic substance. We must be willing to admit that the Absolute is inaccessible to us, and his three modes as well. Moreover, the principle of our individuality is so far removed from him that we could never approach him alone; and that even when aided by him, it takes us eons of years to be capable of gazing upon his face. Hence, our knowledge, or rather our recognition, of the Absolute, and our communion with him, are not really our work, but are the goal or the recompense of our labor. All that our most brilliant geniuses could say are but empty, meaningless words, because the Son alone knows what he is.

The Son, the Word, is Being, and the attribute of Being is life. Thus, everything is alive: a speck of dust, the millionth part of an organic cell, the entire galaxy of stars. Not only are they all alive, but they know that they are alive. All possess intelligence and liberty of action. Of all beings, the Word is the alpha (first) and will be the omega (last). The Word is immovable in his essence, infinite in his aspects. He is the only just, the only splendor, the only reality, because he is always and everywhere the acting, living will of the Father.

What is the *verb* in grammar? It is the part of speech that indicates action. In the cosmos, the *Verb* (that is, the Word) is action. Any creature is an action of God, but the Word is the act par excellence, or rather simply: the Word *is*.

This should make us respect a great many things. If only we had the awareness of this omnipresence of the Word within us, even an inkling of it, we would hesitate to shatter it: the smallest insect would be safe; the earth would not be torn apart without need, nor be overworked; objects would not be wasted for the pleasure of destruction; our brothers would not constantly suffer from our discourteousness.

These thoughts, stemming from profound conviction, are merely geared towards the material order. But is it not more important to live according to the little we know, rather than to run after some new concepts? We have to pay for everything, and the smallest suffering we have inflicted upon anyone will inevitably bounce back to us. So, the man who would decide to follow two or three very simple rules rigorously, what progress he could make! What peace there would be in and about him!

⊕

Why was the name "Word" (Fr. *Verb*) given to the creative agent? Speech is the most perfect mode of expression on earth. To express means to exteriorize, develop, to shove or to thrust out that which is within. A sequence of words forming a logical whole is speech. What does "speak" mean, if not to sow causes? What is creation, if not growth from the center to the circumference: the realization with space and duration of the all: contained by the always, the never, and the nowhere of the Absolute?

The universe is the progressive realization of a thought of the Father. A symphony can remain beautiful as an ideal in the composer's mind, audible only to the inner ear; or else with time and work it may be written down, be given to interpreters, then be performed and repeated hundreds of times in the future. In the imagination of a Bach, for instance, a work exists in its minutest nuances and all its perfections. And yet, the evening of its performance, a musician's ill-will may deform it. So, in the kingdom of the Father, all is in perfect harmony. But if he did not exteriorize himself through his Word, it would be like with the work of a dilettante—no one could experience similar esthetic emotions, or discover within it art, laws, or find a method to create in turn similar sublime harmonies.

If we were to measure how much labor is entailed to produce any kind of work, we would be terrified by the overpowering load that weighs down the shoulders of the Word. To organize the indefinity of time and space, to distribute within it millions of hierarchies of beings, to give to each his task, to make them all compete for the same goal, to be everywhere in order to correct errors, to uplift wilting energies, to restrain follies, and to rectify hideousness—this is the task of the Word, and that is how the immense development of the universe is but the growth of his cosmic body. One understands how the comparisons of the Vedas, of Roman liturgies, and the Kabbalah are realities, rather than symbols. The grand Celestial Man of the ancient sages is not a figurehead; it is a being, just as our body is a universe for the organic atoms that travel therein. Just as the earth is a world to an individual, so this earth and this solar system and the nebula are but physical cells of the great universal whole.

Every creature possesses speech: not only the stones, plants, animals, and the invisible, but objects as well. We do not know these languages, it is true, because we are not yet men. If, perchance, we really knew them, the dignity of our soul would be such that any creature we would speak to would be obliged to obey us, and our lack of wisdom would have grave consequences; this is one of the reasons for our ignorance.

Our speech has a virtue. We can, when we speak, be the cause of acts around us. But our verbal force is quite limited, while the speech of the Father is all-powerful. Hence, before one learns to speak, one must learn the mechanism and the effects of speech. This apprenticeship consists of life, of experience, work, and tests. A student must master the easy lesson first before going on to study the next one.

So, if, from the moment of birth, our physical body had never left its cradle, it would not have developed, nor could we even stand up. The first steps of a child, his first winter, and his first summer, made him suffer, but his organs were fortified by the constant ordeals. It is for an analogous reason that the Father has created darkness, nothingness, and what we call evil. This is what the evangelist means to convey when he says: "The light shines in the darkness."

This light of men, being life, it follows that darknesses are death and immobility, for life is motion. Life and death are constantly at war. Thus, the kingdom of God is not repose, but perpetual motion and total life. In fact, nothing ever stands still. The cry of a beast one million years ago still vibrates somewhere and can still be heard under certain conditions. The monsters of ancient mythologies, the inhabitants of the entrails of the earth, of the ocean bottoms, the beings that fill the air, the antediluvian races, the last of the infusoria, and the first of the gods will always remain alive here or elsewhere. Their energies weigh us down, their emanations suppress or electrify us, their joys or sorrows are communicated to us.

Let us consider ourselves blessed that our eyes are not yet opened, and that, since so many eyes spy upon us, and so many ears eavesdrop, every part of our existence takes on importance. Let us learn how to bring these phantoms,

The Word

these tendencies and desires that are also ours, back to the unique life of Christ, which is ever present, ever on guard, back to the unique light within our very core.

⊕

Christ can then descend into man. His presence ignites the divine spark, which our soul must then nurture—and all the physical substances that clothe it thereby find themselves purified and revivified. For Christ to come into us (and I might add that he is awaiting our permission), we must believe in him. But this simple faith, quite contrary to what the Churches teach, is an enormous task.

Let us add that heaven does everything in its power to encourage us. To anyone who sincerely seeks heaven, Christ sends one proof after another of his action, unless we deliberately keep our eyes closed. Our duty is never to lose one of those intuitions. This in itself is difficult because we must grasp these intuitions on the fly in order to profit by them—but if we are materialistic, we cannot do so.

This comes from the fact, John says, that men come from different roots, consequently they can only reach a limited development during one lifetime.

Those who are born "of the blood," or "of the bloods," are the product of matter, which life always seeks to increase. That kind of child is sent to his parents without their ever having thought of him: it is an automatic reproduction of organic cells linked to circumstances.

Those who are born "of the will of the flesh" are less numerous: they have been directed to one family or other, unbeknownst to the parents, in order to complete a series, to fill a empty place in the terrestrial army, because of their individual destiny, which is divided into periods.

Rare are those who are born "of the will of man." That entails quite rare notions and powers on the part of the parents, the usage of which is not always in conformance with the law.

But, finally, those who come here-below by order of the Father are most rare. They are perfect, reintegrated, missionaries—in short, free men. They serve as models to all other men, whose only resemblance to them is physical. Those have God as father and Truth as mother: their will is divine, their faculties are as pure as their organs. Their whole being is conscious of heaven, regardless of all veils, distances, and time: error, evil, and death hasten away from where they are.

⊕

The incarnation of the Word, as the catechism tells us, is a mystery, something our reason cannot comprehend. In fact, we must not imagine that human mentality can understand everything. Theoretically, it is possible for it to assimilate all that exists in the created or relative realms, all that is measurable, and all life that, similar to itself, is part and function of time, number, and space. Yet, within these limits, there are ideas still too far away for the mind to grasp at present—for instance, there are people unable to comprehend metaphysical premises, and many among the most intelligent may also find some concepts beyond them.

So, that which grows beyond and above the relative state cannot be grasped by the intellect. And intuition coming from the heart permits us to be more or less aware of truth, that is all. When, for example, a man trained in the study of symbolism explains that the dogma of the Trinity signifies the march of the world, that the Father is life, that the Son

The Word

is humankind, and that the Spirit represents the evolutionary force (or any other interpretation you like)—that is but one adaptation of the mystery, not the explanation thereof.

The incarnation of the Word, thus, is one of these mysteries that we will understand as soon as we will have comprehended how the Absolute becomes relative, the eternal temporal, the infinite finite, force matter, the imponderable ponderable... No reasoning can ever prove any of this. We either believe or we do not believe, according to whether the time is ripe or not. Faith produces the consciousness of the divine within our spirit, and no method may ever artificially effect this consciousness. God alone makes himself known, and we cannot reach that state by ourselves. The mystery deepens more and more because, in the Person of Christ, cohabited in perfect union, are the created and the uncreated.

And as indicated in the chain of ideas in the text of St John, Christ has been, throughout nature, the first of the children of God. That which was natural in him—his visible and invisible bodies—was perfect. His bodies were produced by the supreme effort of evolution possible to creation. If when studying him one looks at the man, one believes him to have been an evolved being, an adept. If one looks only at the God in him, one believes him to be a symbol. But in order to really understand him, such as he is, one must see him as man-god, or rather as God-man.

But we cannot understand this duality, this total oneness, because it is the end result of a kind of force opposite to ours. We exist only to grow, while the Word came down from Absolute life into conditioned life as a sacrifice.

In the plane of oneness, as soon as the Father has expressed his will, it is accomplished by the Son. The incarnation has always been since all eternity, but it has not been realized, is not and will not be realized upon the innumerable temporal orbs (which means upon all visible and invisible planets) except at different moments in time. In order for this miracle to occur in a created organism at a certain point of space, it is necessary that there be a conjunction of this point with the divine central sphere. This is one of the meanings of the sign of the cross. Hence, it is necessary that the life, the spirit, and the personality of this planet, when grappling with some "impossible," turn back towards the center of the universe as towards salvation. The same conjunction is indispensable for the descent of the Word into an individual. He dwells within the realm of souls, since the beginning, and he will so dwell forever. But for this sojourn of his to be felt by the conscience in travail of one or another of these souls, it is necessary that their temporary bodies, through moral purification and repentance, move into the axis of the radiation of their creator.

Through the following examples I would like to make you understand the mode of propagation of the movements of the unity. From the center of the universe (though in reality there is neither center, top, nor bottom), the movements that occur reverberate more or less fast and more or less integral upon one or another focus according to the state of this focus. So, let us just imagine an observer situated on the sun. This observer has a special measure of time: he would see the incarnation of the Word take place on earth in the year 2000 according to his solar chronology, or in the year 800 upon Mercury, and the year 10000 upon Saturn, etc. Another observer, at the constellation of Hercules, would have analogous differences, but on a vaster scale; and so forth.

The Word

This gross image will help you, I hope, to understand that time and space are multiple; but that where there is no matter anymore, neither is there number. At that level, all is everywhere, actual, and simultaneous.

⊕

"The Word lives among us full of grace and truth," says St John. It is thus that he explains the dual nature of Christ: the perfect human and the complete divine united. The individual personality of Christ is perfect only in order to offer his divine entity a perfect working tool. In other words, Christ is ideal man: the intermediary and the intercessor between the created and the uncreated. From all points of the universe, he gathers together all the aspirations of all beings for heaven, and he pours divine help upon them all.

That is why he possesses the plenitude of grace and also that of truth. Grace is something very mysterious. It is an impalpable, imperceptible, and unseizable force even for adepts. It goes everywhere, penetrates everything; we are able only to apprehend its effects. The help we receive for the fulfillment of filial, domestic, social, or professional duties is usually but the collaboration of certain attendants invisible to man—because these duties are of general importance, and the spirit of our earth (only to mention our planet) is interested in their having truly synchronized. This help is not grace; neither are the ordinary motivations for our activity. Plainly speaking, one's desires are but the manifestation of the evolutive force that Hermeticists refer to as the elements and stars: everything has a tendency to increase in nature—matter, vitality, magnetism, the cerebral, psychic, and soul faculties, etc.

Grace, on the contrary, comes from above and not from below: it descends only to reascend with us, while evolution brings us to a zenith only to bring us down to a relative nadir. Let us keep our study within the framework of this earth. Before the Word incarnated here, the earth was only acting in concert with the rest of creation; it could not develop past a certain point. Neither could its inhabitants. Both could expect help only from superior beings or from higher planes—but always within the orbs of destiny. They too only had the personal force of propagation that they received along with existence. Thus it is that muscular energy cannot keep on developing in an individual indefinitely, unless someone could change his physical life. This extraordinary intervention, which is supernatural in the ontological sense of the word, is called grace.

All the substances imaginable that God can send in multiples are comprised in that word "grace"; these substances, when assimilated by planetary atmospheres and individual organisms, can appear to us under very diverse forms, such as metals, liquids, stars, plants, intellectual, psychic, verbal, or thaumaturgical faculties, etc. We cannot know their essence, but we may have an intuition about their origin. This grace is "the water of eternal life"; but for it to reach us, someone had to dig a canal: this is one of the effects of the incarnation of the Word.

So, this succor sent by the Father when one of his children, after having done everything to extricate himself, finds himself still reduced to extremities—this help, since it comes from the Father, always produces there where it has been granted the greatest good compatible to the circumstances. Hence, it is true that grace, given by the Father, transmitted by the Son, is a breath of the Holy Spirit. And

The Word

this unseizable air, whose inbreathing produces within us the seven gifts indicated in our catechism, has the distinctive characteristic of liberty—and the final result of its visit is to give us our liberation.

Hence, the Word incarnate is really, as described by John, "filled with grace and truth," since he came to effect the ultimate cure upon creation by bringing to it truth, which is the seed of its future liberty.

For man there is but one truth, towards which all science is aimed: to acknowledge the law of the world. The invisible is always teaching us the articles of the law that regulate our work for the moment. This notion is called conscience. When we disobey it, we are forging for ourselves a chain for the future. That is how error and captivity are synonymous and lean towards matter, while truth and freedom are of the spirit. Wisdom, intelligence, counsel, strength, science, piety, and the fear of God are, as we know, the seven fruits that the Holy Spirit ripens within us, as they have been defined so often by the Roman doctors and the mystics of all schools. You will easily recall these speculations—though they encompass but a small part of the developments of truth (verity) within the soul. In order to explain the gifts of the Holy Spirit one would have to possess them in their plenitude. But you who have studied ancient wisdoms, ancient esotericisms, you are able to judge their amplitude by the very amplitude that their ancient books attribute to the perfect adept.

Immediate perception of what has to be done; the comprehension of any state of soul, the faculty of giving to each what he needs; the consciousness of our nothingness, the perception of truth in all things, the faculty of praying; absolute submission to the Father—these are the seven periphrases that may explain the ordinary names given to the gifts of the Spirit.

The last words of verse 14 need explanation. To be precise, the apostles and disciples, all those who have believed, who now believe, and who will believe in Christ, Son of God, have seen nothing but his glory. One cannot stare straight into the sun at midday, but one may see its rays. The sun of souls, the Word, also sends out rays, which are nothing but the appearance he assumes depending upon the planes he crosses through and the creatures whom he addresses. The higher the plane has evolved, the more saintly is the spectator, and the more numerous will the visible radiations be. But no one will ever see the Son face to face, such as he is, prior to the final reintegration. For each of the innumerable rays that form his aureole or glory is alive with a life of its own, though freely obedient; each is a fragmentary aspect of the ineffable Being from which it emanates. That explains how, when saints speak of having seen such and such a divine Person—and they are sincere—what they have seen is but an aspect of that Person that is compatible with their own limitation.

But let us leave these too rare exceptions aside. The majority of those who simply feel that God hides himself behind the sweet figure of Christ are capable of that intuition only because some part of them, as the evangelist says, has seen the glory of the Only Son. This illumination probably took place far away from here, maybe in some of the visible worlds, even perhaps in the invisible. We may also have seen the Messiah two thousand years ago somewhere on earth; we may have seen him since; we may not know it at the present time. But if we feel his divinity, though doubt, erudition, and despair may stand in our way at times, that little spark will always burn in the bottom of our heart, with a steady and immutable flame.

The inner always has command over the outer; men and nature, left to themselves, can only become perfected from the outer to the inner, from the denser to the lighter, from the solid to the fluidic. On the other hand, heaven, which is the center of everything, acts upon the center of everyone, heals beings by treating them from the inner to the outer, from the spiritual to the material.

God and creatures also go to meet each other; but the Father takes long strides, while his children loiter on the way. So it is the Father who in reality makes the meeting possible, since the very strength his children use to walk there, comes from him. Let us never forget this. Let us never forget that our life does not belong to us, that we must give it as gratuitously as it was given us; and that this gift, no matter how painful it may be, is necessary if we want to have advanced on the road of life before death overtakes us.

The Birth of
the Word Within Us

HE BIRTH of the Word within us is nothing but having the certitude of individual salvation. It is eternal beatitude realized on earth, infinite liberty being reconquered, the triumph of love, and peace enthroned on the apex of our heart. Reams have been written about this theme. But, faithful to our habit of direct contemplation, we will not bother about what former commentators have said before us, so as to have the field free to our current intuition. Later, if time remains, we will compare our study with the old texts, in order to rectify or complete it. Primarily, we must define the true new birth, then search for its preparatory phenomena, describe this birth as best can be, examine how the Word grows in us, and finally, conclude with practical indications.

Let us remember that within us there are the eternal soul, or dormant germ of the Absolute, and the immortal spirit, whose works reactivate the soul, awaken and furnish it with the necessary food to make it grow and keep its flame alive. This is one of the aspects of the conflagration that Christ was so anxious to see lit. It is this combustion that produces the mystical growth of God within us.

The avenue by which our soul is held to the Father is this

The Birth of the Word Within Us

very same Christ, who, living in the Absolute, lives simultaneously in the relative—and primarily in us. The inner Virgin is the avenue by which the soul spreads into the visible and invisible organisms of an individual. But here, as everywhere, the two are one: Son giving life to his Mother; the Mother giving her Son her substance, her life.

The historical event of the birth of Jesus has been associated with astronomy (St Gregory of Nyssa, St Augustine, Volney, Dupuis), with astrology (F. Delaulnaye), with alchemy (Madathanus, Pernety), with cosmology (the Vedas, the Greek poets, Prudence), with psychology (St Leon's sixth sermon on Christmas, the Venerable Bede, Father Gratry). The Christian mystics, even the Protestants such as Jacob Boehme, teach that when Christ is born in us, the soul must undergo similar pains and pass through situations analogous to those he has suffered.

But we must note that true mystical birth is a very rare miracle. Mere baptism does not procure it. The Salvation Army and Protestants who believe themselves regenerated by simply repenting are also wrong. It is impossible for the light to increase in us if darkness reigns therein, because many of the visible and invisible beings could not breathe the too rarefied atmosphere of heaven without dying, and the responsibilities that such illumination entails would crush ordinary shoulders.

The initiations of ancient wisdom, which are still extant in our day, clearly speak of a new birth; in fact, they promise their neophytes the privilege of seeing an invisible world. But it is only one among thousands of worlds; while Christic regeneration opens the door to the unique, eternal, and supernatural kingdom of God. Please note this essential difference.

THE CHILDHOOD OF JESUS

Let us look at Catholicism. There are two Catholicisms: that of the crowds and that of the contemplatives. Only the latter are preoccupied with mystical rebirth. Permit me to speak a little bit about our religion.

According to theology, *mysticism* is uniquely concerned with extraordinary states of consciousness for which the will has no bearing upon their attainment, as they are a pure gift from God; whereas *asceticism* is the method by which the devout makes himself capable of receiving these graces and of withstanding them.

On the ordinary path, one progresses mainly by action, though it is grace that gives us the strength to act; on the mystical path, it is by means of contemplation.

To be impartial, I must add that in spite of the idea of supremacy that theologians attach to contemplative life, a few Doctors teach that to attain perfect union with the divine is not irreconcilable with a mere laic type of life.

There are three major schools among Catholic asceticisms. The Dominican, which is mainly intellectual and philosophical; the Franciscan, which is emotional and soulful; and the Jesuit, which is volitive. Nevertheless, all three possess the same great principles integrally.

Though I have repugnance in mentioning some of my mental reservations regarding the teachings of the Church, I must say that the regeneration she offers us is still but partial, since it encompasses only that portion of the human being incarnated upon earth, while true regeneration extends over the total being.

This is a venturous theory, at least for the moment, but it may someday become part of the dogma. Let us remember that St Bernard had already proclaimed the Immaculate Conception, but that it took seven centuries for this con-

The Birth of the Word Within Us

templative's intuition to become an article of faith (by Pope Pius IX in 1854).

As a word of warning, let us note that regeneration constitutes a very dangerous process if we force it upon someone who is not ready. It demands, in fact, purity of the entire being. It means that all our physical cells, and every atom of all of our invisible bodies, must have gone through necessary trials and accomplished their task. This represents a great many physical illnesses, intellectual anguish, and moral suffering—which calls for multiple lives.

This regeneration is neither something cultivated, nor the refinement or sublimation of our faculties. It is a graft, a transplantation, a transmutation. Everything must die within us, so that all might be reborn. The very root of our will and of our individualism must be transformed.

Ancient wisdom had to be conquered through desperate combats against some kind of formidable and cunning guardian; remember the Thebaic crypts, the Brahmanic caverns, and the pit of Raguel. Today, living knowledge can be obtained when, leaning on the breast of our Friend, shielded by the ramparts of his merciful arms, we see the worlds, from the infinitely large to the infinitely small, passing by.

We merely glanced over at the processes preparatory to regeneration, when we covered the Precursor. In the gospel, the personages as well as the localities exist within us, not as symbols, but as psychic organs activated by spiritual faculties. Thus the ascending ternary of Zacharias, Elizabeth, and John the Baptist is coupled to the descending ternary of Joseph, Mary, and Jesus. The first three persons are:

Zacharias (penance), Elizabeth (action), John the Baptist (repentance). The other three are: Joseph (the carrying of the cross), Mary (renunciation), Jesus (the imitation of Christ). The first ternary is our spirit ascending to the soul; the second is our soul descending to the spirit.

Let us be content with these summary examples.

Though each man carries the light within himself, he has to feed it so that it may transmute the organisms that surround him. But almost always, instead of feeding, we smother the light which, during numerous lives, remains foreign to and hidden from us. We sustain the very life that is in us with the corrupt substances of cupid selfishness, with the venomous odors of matter, instead of subjecting them to the purifying action of the light by our practicing virtues.

The evangelist very justly states that darkness does not want any of the light hidden in its bosom, and that the world does not understand it, though it is he who has built it. The house does not know its architect.

That light is the Word: the Word of the Father that vivifies everything, even giving to evil men the force they use to hit him. He especially speaks through the voice of the conscience, though we obstinately turn a deaf ear. He nourishes the soul. Because, if, each time we satisfy a selfish whim, we cheat another being, we cause trouble, vengeance, and pain for the future—while if, on the contrary, we listen to the Word's voice with our center, if we sacrifice our inclinations, the milieu receives benefits therefrom and we advance one step further towards harmony: we imitate the work of the Father and become capable of greater beatitude.

The same explanations hold good for the history of a race as for that of the whole of humankind.

The Birth of the Word Within Us

So that the Word may descend to re-light within each individual man the dying spark, there has to be a conjunction of the spiritual center of that man with the divine center: the self, vanquished by the impossible, must turn back with a desperate effort towards the One for whom there is no impossible. The sign of the cross represents this meeting in the universe, in the zodiac, upon each planet.

The Word dwells in the world of souls also, since the beginning, and forever; but for his presence to be felt, it is necessary that our bodies—envelopes of the soul—reinstall themselves within the axis of divine radiation through repentance, moral purification, and charity.

When a man gives heaven the opportunity to descend, prior to the incarnation during which the mystery of this descent is to be celebrated, the Holy Spirit hovers over the human spirit, so that when the soul joins with the personality, the latter is frightened in turn of the soul's personality, and needs to be reassured by an angel, just as Gabriel convinced Joseph to keep Mary, despite appearances. It has to be so, because no matter how exalted these persons, selves, or wills may be, they are still far from the purity of the spirit.

From the standpoint of the soul, in order for Christ to be born, it is essential for our individuality (Joseph), and for this still unknown faculty one calls imagination (in the deepest sense of the word)—which have been active and powerful so far—to have recognized their unworthiness, and to be brought back to their original root, back to the state in which they were when they began to work. When they will have become exhausted, when they will be unable to do anything but wait, when they will not find any nourishment in their activity—then, one night, the Word will be born. It is the Virgin within who takes care of him;

while the individuality (Joseph), the physical faculties (the ox), and the sensorial faculties (the donkey) remain passive and powerless.

Our meeting with the Bridegroom may take place: by means of the intention with which we endow our actions; by our renunciation; or by the annihilation of the self. But this meeting always occurs in the deepest night.

Yet we must see in spite of that darkness.

What will light our path? Three lights, corresponding to the three modes of the meeting: the grace of God, forgetting created images, and renunciation to the self.

Through the third light, the Bridegroom enters into the heart; through the second, he enters the intellectual soul; but it is through the first that he enters the superconscious oneness of our spirit.

⊕

Taken in the individual sense, the shepherds represent the nervous system of vegetal life, which watches over the functioning of our physical organism day and night, and which, at the time of divine illumination, is renovated, purified, and energized. The magi-kings represent the conscious nervous system, Herod the will. The star is mental intuition; Bethlehem is the stable; the night of the nativity brings the three essential privations. The ox and the donkey are, as we said before, the physical and sensorial faculties of corporal life.

In reality, nothing happens to us haphazardly. There are always signs that foretell visits or events. He alone, the Word, enters into us, installs himself without anyone being able to foretell the miraculous moment, because he alone among all beings depends upon no circumstances. He is

The Birth of the Word Within Us

free. This is demonstrated to us by the star, the angels, and especially by the refusal of men at large to welcome their Savior.

But, in order to excuse them, let us say that to receive the Word is hardly a simple event.

When friends are coming for a visit, in their honor we clean house; but the different apartments of which man is composed are far more difficult to clean. The body has to be purified first; secondly the spirit, which is so complex; and then the almost impalpable envelope of the soul.

To receive the Word into our body does not mean to have eliminated such and such chemical atoms through any special, strict diet; it means having vanquished evil within our organic molecules. In fact, man is a whole whose parts are tightly coordinated. In him, sensation reacts upon feelings and his intellect, and each of these two react upon others. So, when thought, feeling, or action contain evil, the physical organism is vitiated much more deeply than through a lack of hygiene; to purify this organism, one must first purify one's desires.

To receive Christ into our electro-vital body, does not mean to subject our nervous system to the disciplinary training of occult sciences. It means to make it capable of accomplishing all sorts of tasks, and to force it to surmount any antipathies it meets in the world of bodies.

To receive Christ in our magnetic body, means giving up the ways of the magician who realizes the *noli ire, fac venire* ("Do not go, let them come") of Eliphas Lévi. It means abandoning the attitude of one who, fighting for recognition, wants to dominate—as do the modern sectarians of "personal magnetism." It means abandoning the still more dangerous attitude of the one who sits immobile, and who tries to kill all desire or movement within himself. On the contrary, it means to so forget oneself that one never expects any recompense for the good one has done.

To receive Christ within our astral body means abandoning the cult of the gods in order to consecrate oneself to the cult of God.

To receive Christ in our soul body, or sentient body, means to cultivate indulgence, compassion, and charity.

To receive Christ in our mental body means to purify science and thought; it means never to use them for evil or for personal advantage; it means to regard them as unreliable and powerless as long as they are founded only upon knowledge of one of nature's fragments.

To receive Christ in our will, in the self, means that it can happen only when the self is dead, when we have become indifferent to any act per se; or, if you prefer, when everything that comes along is for us a joy because it gives us the joy of obeying, of doing the Father's will, regardless of the inconveniences it may cause us.

Finally, for our spirit to receive Christ, means that total and essential poverty must have been attained. Later, we will see what it consists of.

In short, we are free; free to welcome the light or to chase it away. It is true that, depending upon our past and our destiny, the future may require of us one thing or another. There even comes a time when we cannot shoulder the accumulation of the consequences of our acts any more. But if we ask for help, not in a complaining manner, but fighting for all we are worth, heaven heeds our call and sends us help.

To refuse the light—which we too often do—comes as a consequence of what the Hindu calls karma. It results from

The Birth of the Word Within Us

natural filiations that do not correspond to the spiritual ones anymore. Physiologically, a child is certainly the son of his physical father and mother, but often, very often, his spirit differs from theirs; and this disparity weakens us for the fight.

The growth of Christ within us is analogous, though yet dissimilar, to any biological development. It entails joys and sorrows, both suffered in silence; it is nothing but the construction of the glory-body, of which the Holy Spirit fills the role of architect—on condition that the new man gives him full and constant collaboration through love of suffering. Then the divine ferment destroys everything within us in order to reorganize everything, with pure elements, upon a new plane.

The courage one needs to abandon all former laid-out roads comes from the call of the Word. Each step we take comes only through the indescribable force of this call. Successively, the traveler abandons his cloak, his shoes, his stick—which were indispensable when he followed the highway, but are superfluous now that he climbs the solitary by-ways. The rarefied air of the virgin regions he traverses even changes the quality of his blood. His strength augments through the ascents, the descents, and the dives into the rivers; the awareness of danger keys up his senses. Just as physical labors borne for a noble ideal ennoble the character, so the constant preoccupation of nourishing nothing but the soul, of giving it nothing but the one food suited to it—God (meaning, by sacrifice)—finally results in transfiguring and sublimating the entire personality of the intrepid voyager.

If during this long voyage we try to find some landmarks, we will find them in an adaptation of the events related in

THE CHILDHOOD OF JESUS

the gospels. Thus, the massacre of the innocents represents the death of the physical cells that nourished the fire of the soul. The flight into Egypt represents this fire penetrating into the most corrupt centers of the personality. The unknown adolescence of Christ is the silent mystery in which the inner "great work" is accomplished. The temptations, the baptism, the miracles, the sermons, the passion and the death of Christ, are just so many dramas where the regenerated one will play the principal role before re-entering at last into the peace of his Lord.

The persons of the gospel, the apostles, the holy women, the pontiffs, the sick, all represent spiritual forces. I prefer not giving any details upon these points, for fear of indiscretions, and to prevent the possible digressions of searchers who are more enthusiastic than prudent. There are in any event already so few whose spirit is strong enough to withstand these upheavals.

We have finally reached the end of the cycle of the childhood of Christ. You who have been willing to listen to me to the end, and you, too, who did not stop after having read the first pages of this book, it is good for you to know that, because we have one solicitude in common, the most noble of all solicitudes, we are united by an invisible yet real link—elastic perhaps, but nevertheless impossible to break. A true group needs no forms, nor statutory laws. It exists at the very moment when wills become allied, and it persists as long as their goal lasts. For us, our aim is immutable.

To know that inwardly you might be associated with unknown people whose characters, opinions, or social posi-

The Birth of the Word Within Us

tions might displease you, were you to meet them, should not cause you any misgivings: on the contrary, since that uncertainty is a possible cause for even more intense works.

Accept this as the only proof you are able to offer our Friend for the encouragements he gives you. Think of all the centuries he has worn himself out for us! If you only knew what pure joy he feels from our efforts! How, for him, our lively spirits, our spontaneities, exude perfume! We are a flock led to green pastures. Know that we will remain together as long as you care to remain. Know that the Shepherd watches us from a hilltop reddened by the flowers of tribulations. Know that his mysterious watchdogs protect and defend us. Let us advance into ineffable joy, in the silent inebriation of light, into this ambience of powerful kindness and peace that the hope of our Master sheds all around.

It is in this essential space, where in an incomprehensible manner all things remain eternally present, that the soul remains near her Lord, her Bridegroom, her Friend. Finally, having had to undergo hardships and tribulations together, the soul body and the radiant bodies of the Word unite, are grafted together, as they go throughout the various realms of this nature welded as one, in and by the dazzling flame of their mutual love.

This is the beatitude I wish for you from the depths of my heart.

The Childhood

HEN HEROD, when he saw he had been mocked by the magi, became very angry, and ordered that all children of Bethlehem and the surroundings from two years old and under be put to death, reckoning the time which he had diligently inquired of the wise men. It was then that the word spoken by the prophet Jeremiah was fulfilled: In Rama, was heard a voice, lamentations and mourning. It was Rachel weeping for her children. She would not be comforted as there were none left. (Matthew 2:16–18)

In order to prevent Herod from accomplishing his criminal projects, the magi received a vision. An angel appeared to Joseph, and the holy family fled into Egypt. These first tribulations of Christ as a child were already the result of his sacrifice. He could, in fact, have chosen happiness, wealth, and shown himself to humans as the supreme prototype of intellectual and political glory. On the contrary, his purpose was to travel the most arduous roads of poverty, pain, humiliation, ingratitude, doubt; in a word, to shoulder all imaginable tribulations, in order to show us, when the time comes, how we must bear and overcome them.

Regarding the massacre of the innocents, legend has exaggerated it. Bethlehem and its adjoining territory only had from two to three thousand inhabitants, and the children below the age of two could hardly have exceeded

The Childhood

twenty. Matthew, who continues to quote the prophets, since he addressed himself especially to the Jews, recalls Jeremiah in this instance. The Father always tries to prevent his children's blood from being shed; but when things reach this extremity, it is always the stubborn perversity of creatures that is responsible

On the other hand, everything is relative; and if you have ever thought that mineral life (though quite miraculous) is still well beneath mental life, so the life of Christ—perfect archetype of man, the king of creation—was far more precious than even that of a thousand ordinary children. Finally, these were victims only because of the loss of their physical body; but on the spiritual plane, they received a great advancement. It was the souls of these little children, who, right after the death of Jesus, re-embodied as disciples. One needs not find out whether they were really innocent or if their immolation had been merited.

After the departure of the magi-kings, an angel of the Lord appeared to Joseph in a dream, saying: Arise, take the child and his mother and flee into Egypt, where you will remain until I send you word; for Herod will seek the child to destroy him. That same night Joseph arose, he took the child and his mother and departed into Egypt, where he remained until the death of Herod, in fulfillment of the word which the Lord spoke by his prophet: I called my Son out of Egypt. When Herod was dead, an angel of the Lord appeared to Joseph in Egypt in a dream and said, Arise, take the child and his mother and go into the land of Israel, for

THE CHILDHOOD OF JESUS

those who sought his life are dead: Joseph then arose, took the child and his mother and returned to the land of Israel. (Matthew 2:13–15; 19–21)

The apocryphal gospels abound in details regarding the sojourn of Jesus in Egypt; they relate miraculous events. It is a fact that Jesus, as a mere child, already exerted his power, at least within the measure that his physical organism could withstand the fulgurant presence of his divinity.

Remember that the Word, when he incarnated, accepted the chains of matter in all the departments of his being. His social activities and his biological faculties could only perform after a long period of accommodation. The body he had built for himself was constructed out of the purest parts of physical substance. This selection was necessary, because the powers of the spirit are a devouring fire to matter, and an ordinary organic substance could not withstand them: it would merely volatize at their contact. That is why the body of Christ was perfect from all standpoints, and also why several years were needed to accustom all the cells to become complete instruments of theurgic forces that were constantly passing through them. This is the natural training to which Luke made allusions, by repeating twice: "Jesus grew in wisdom, in stature, and grace before God and men."

In fact, just as seeds grow in opposite directions: root and stem, so man also—or rather his vital center, his spiritual heart—grows in two opposite directions: towards heaven and towards earth: then the individual's equilibrium as well as his total health are realized only when the obscure roots sink into tribulations and work; then the spiritual fruits and flowers, though invisible to our earthly eyes at present, abound with life.

The Childhood

We, too, must grow before men through work, energy, constancy, and charity; and also grow before God through humility, prayer, and faith.

⊕

Every year, his parents used to go to Jerusalem for the Feast of the Passover. When he was twelve years old, they went up to Jerusalem, as was the custom. After completing the days of its observance, they returned, but the boy Jesus tarried in Jerusalem, though his parents were unaware of it. But they, thinking he was among their traveling companions, had gone a whole day's journey before making inquiry among their kinsfolk and acquaintances. When they could not find him, they returned to Jerusalem, in search of him, and it was only after three days that they found him in the Temple, seated among the doctors, both listening to them and asking them questions. All those who heard him were astonished at his understanding and the answers he gave. When they saw him there, they were full of wonder, and his mother said to him: My Son, why did you act that way towards us? Your father and I have sought you in great anguish. He answered: What reason had you to search for me? Did you not know I must attend to my Father's business? His parents did not understand the words he used. He went down with them to Nazareth and remained subject to them while his mother kept the memory of these things in her heart; and Jesus advanced in wisdom and stature and in grace before God and before men. (Luke 2:41–52)

THE CHILDHOOD OF JESUS

Joseph is always portrayed to us as the model of ordinary man in whom the powers of the Spirit have never been overtly manifested. He works for his family, obeys civil and religious laws; he follows the indications given him by the Invisible in a most common manner through dreams; he says little, but he acts; and finally he dies, as he has lived, in obscurity.

The holy family, when it left Egypt, came back to settle in Nazareth—not in Judea, but in Galilee, thus fulfilling another prophecy. The Jews called the children who were consecrated to the Lord from their youth Nazareans. The verb *natzer* in Hebrew means "to flourish"; *natzir* means "consecrated."

So, from the point of view of the Invisible, the consecrated child must give his intelligence, his life, and all his faculties to God. In exchange, this gift then procures for him the efflorescence of a special light suited to the individual and to the needs of the moment.

Thus, the child reached his twelfth year; and it was during one of these trips which Joseph and Mary made yearly to Jerusalem that they lost him for three days, only to find him in the Temple teaching the doctors of Israel.

The symbolic applications of this episode are easily explained. First of all, let us note that the first public act of Christ is addressed to the spiritual leaders of the people, to the scholars, to the intellectuals, and to the political leaders in Israel. The wisdom of the prodigious child represents but a curious case to their erudition or scepticism; but this attempt to enlighten the upper classes had to be made—there again, Jesus was conforming to the established ideas of the social order.

Yet he does not have one solitary word of consolation for

The Childhood

his parents: and in a few other circumstances one sees him keep his distance, because (and we must not forget it) no matter how great be the praise that Catholicism grants to the parents of Jesus, no matter how much they towered above the highest level of humanity, Joseph and Mary are nevertheless far behind the divine humanity of their Son. We are hardly aware of this difference, just as when twelve miles away we are unable to gauge the exact height of adjoining mountains: and the further away they are, the less we can distinguish the difference in height of their summits.

We must remember (though it seems unbelievable) that the parents of Jesus did not have a precise idea of his identity, nor of the mission of their Son. They were two beings, as pure and perfect as human nature can fashion perfection; but, as we just mentioned, they had not understood the import of the marvels they were living through. They could not, of themselves, understand. Indeed, it was imperative that they should not know—as much to enable Jesus to live the state of soul of misunderstood children, as to offset the spies of invisible darkness.

Let us view these various episodes as glorifications of obedience. St Ambrose of Milano detects two causes at the basis of the constant revolt of man: his pride and his cowardice. His pride makes him stand up to God; his cowardice makes him shirk his duties. The Virgin teaches us how to neutralize these two troubles: the highest among beings submits to the law better than the least ever would; the purest among women accepts the dagger of inner martyrdom better than the greatest criminal ever would. And by her side, her Son realizes supernatural obedience above all, just as he justifies his comforting declaration in advance: "I came to fulfill the law, not to destroy it."

Just as St Augustine, the Bishop of Hippo, stated, the Lord did not want his religion to be inaugurated through any dispensation, no matter how legitimate.

Adonai tells his people: Give me your firstborn, because all things belong to me. Jesus, the Man-Jesus, is the perfect creature, the ideal upon whom, from the beginning to the end of the universe, all eyes are focused. And he is the firstborn of the Father. He is the perfect holocaust, the perfect sacrifice, the perfect sacerdote—all three eternal, universal, permanent.

This child in the manger, in the arms of the priest, in the house of Nazareth, is the example of the most radical and unreasonable submission: that is what the divine incongruity of love is. Out of gratitude should we not challenge reason by efforts of renunciation?

Obedience is the primary class in the school of renunciation. It is more fruitful than all physical asceticisms and contemplations. In it are hidden the secrets of the freedom of the spirit, on condition that we observe it even if it seems unreasonable to common sense. However, these are no edicts that state one must submit to any immoral orders. Since no one fills a role unless God has permitted it, we must create within ourselves a state of joyous and instantaneous submission. Besides, to anyone who has dedicated himself totally to God, nothing can ever happen unless it has been expressly willed by the Father.

⊕

Joseph, having learned that Archelaus was reigning in Judea in the place of his father Herod, feared to return there. Receiving warning in a dream, he left for a prov-

The Childhood

ince in Galilee and settled in a city called Nazareth, so that what the prophets had spoken might be fulfilled: He shall be called a Nazarene. (Matthew 2:22–23)

When all the requirements of the law of the Lord had been accomplished, they returned to Galilee, to their own city of Nazareth. The child grew and came to his strength full of wisdom; and the grace of God rested upon him. (Luke 2:39–40)

Here, Christ teaches us that each time the Father gives us an order, we must execute it, in spite of everything, in spite of family or society. And Luke, a little later, writes of him: "He was subject to his parents in all things." In ordinary life, we must obey everything and all. You probably understand it, but let me repeat that the orders of the Father are rare indeed. There is perhaps but one man per century who receives a mission from the Father. For us, our lot is to serve, to heed the calls, and to never refuse to help. In other words, each has his duty. The missionary has the exceptional duty of deeply moving such or such a corner of the world: for us, the task is the daily and ordinary fare.

The aforementioned words of Luke contain for orthodox teaching the whole history of Jesus from his twelfth to thirtieth year. Some people claim, basing themselves upon superficial findings of oriental archeology, such as those that were published towards the end of the Second Empire by rationalist Freemasons, that Jesus was initiated in India during those eighteen years. I have already stated that this thesis is false; otherwise Jesus would merely be a "Son of God" and not the Incarnated Word.

The indication that Jesus "grew in wisdom and grace" does not signify that he followed an esoteric school. Jesus only took the trouble of being born on earth in order to pass through all the experiences that are the usual condition of man. Hence, he had to be educated, to be taught, subjected to youth, adolescence, and all the vagaries of physiological, temperamental, and mental developments. His divine nature certainly could have built for itself a perfect organism all at once, but then the physical life of the human species could never have received the light of the Spirit. It is this submission of Jesus to all the slow growths of terrestrial life that in the end permitted the latter to receive eternal life.

Yet, there are some people who know what Christ really did during this period; but, since what we would learn thereupon would only satisfy our curiosity and resuscitate controversies, we will leave these matters aside.

That is also what Christ recommends when he speaks of the "secret room" where he invites us to lock ourselves in and join him: he, living and active truth; he, upon whom I beg you to keep your eyes focused; he who, someday—but one day certainly—will let us reach the root of all ideas and the summit of all sentiments.

Conclusion

OUR STUDY of the first part of the gospels is at an end. Some might be surprised that I seemed stingy with details concerning the period of the childhood of Christ properly speaking. There are certain things that must remain mysterious. Yes, all will have to be explained someday, but we are not yet at the end of the world. First we must prevent premature lights; then we must be careful that these lights not be grasped and then perverted by the spies of the Adversary. The massacre of the innocents, the flight into Egypt, the meeting with the doctors, the whole youth of Jesus, are but the material forms of spiritual acts of primary importance still beyond the grasp of our intellect. Let us try not to merely feed our curiosity. It would be an inner gluttony, more disastrous than that of a gourmand. Our brain is already overfed. That is one reason for our disequilibrium. In order to have the right to learn new arcana, we should first of all have fulfilled the majority of the duties that our present knowledge entails. It is especially on the narrow path that the ancient axiom "make haste slowly" should be observed. As St Vincent de Paul (in whom common sense reached a level of genius) said, God does not ask of us to do many things, but to do thoroughly the little we are able to do.

Please note that I am not against the use, even an intensive use, of our intellectual faculties, but against the abuse of their dilapidation. Let us cultivate ourselves in depth, not on the surface. Truth is to be found in the depths: in the pit of Raguel, in the crypts of Dakshinamurthi, in the abysses of mysticism—here are her palaces. Dante himself knew this mystery.

www.ingramcontent.com/pod-product-compliance
Lightning Source LLC
Chambersburg PA
CBHW030105170426
43198CB00009B/499